Love Sells

How to Get Every Home Buyer to Fall in Love with your House

By Karen Schaefer

Simple Appeal® LLC Copyright © 2012 by Karen Schaefer

All rights reserved. No part of this book may be used or reproduced in any manner whatsoever without written permission from Karen Schaefer, except as provided by the United States of America copyright law or in the case of brief quotations embodied in articles and reviews.
The scanning, uploading and distribution of this book via the Internet or via any other means without the permission of the publisher is illegal and punishable by law.

ISBN- 13: 978-1479177219
ISBN- 10: 1479177210

Please purchase only authorized electronic editions and do not participate in or encourage electronic piracy of copyrighted materials. Your support of the author's rights is sincerely appreciated.

Printed in the United States of America

First Printing: 2012

LoveSellsBook.com
by Karen Schaefer

Additional Trainings by Karen Schaefer

Certified Home Stager

Advanced Home Stager

Stager Pro

Property Scene Designer

Home Stager Trainer

Master Trainer

Color Analysis Specialist

37 Point Curb Appeal Specialist

How to Market Your Home Staging Business

Vacant and Distress Staging

STAGE Business and Marketing Training Event

---

www.APSDmembers.com

Dedication

This book is dedicated to my husband Pete Treloar. He is the salt of the earth. He has lifted me up when I have fallen, held me to task when he knew I had it in me, and recognized each of my steps as a step toward success. There is no greater influence in my life than this amazing man and it is because of him that I was able to write this book. Thanks Lovey!

Table of Contents

Page

Table of Contents.. 6

Introduction... 7

Chapter One: *How to create Love in your home* 11

Chapter Two: *Selling in the Shortest Amount of Time for the Most Amount of Money*.. 37

Chapter Three: *The Art of Prepping to Sell*............................. 53

Chapter Four: *Staging with Love*... 78

Chapter Five: *Love at First Sight*... 90

Chapter Six: *Let's Create Brake-Stopping Curb Appeal*........ 103

Chapter Seven: *Staging the Kitchen with Love*...................... 121

Chapter Eight: *Staging Your Bedrooms with Love*................ 131

Chapter Nine: *Staging Your Living Areas with Love*............ 144

Chapter Ten: *Staging Your Bathrooms with Love*.................. 150

Chapter Eleven: *Leaving with Love*....................................... 159

Chapter Twelve: *Resources & Checklists*............................... 162

Introduction

There are 3 things that must happen for your home to sell in the shortest amount of time for the most amount of money. And while, yes, price can sell a house, do you really want to sell it to? Or would you prefer to sell yours for what it is worth?

 Your 3 keys to home selling success:
1) It must be **marketed effectively**, consistently and to the right customer
2) **Brake-Stopping Curb Appeal** should capture the prospects attention and simply compel them to want to see this property
3) **Captivating and Interactive home staging** for the specific buyer with of course, lots of **LOVE**.

Life is not fair. We have experienced that and now the real estate market, the economy and the world is proving it to us. No matter how great your home is, chances are it won't sell fast.

It used to be that we could rely upon 'location, location, location' but let's face facts, today we are so worried about 'vocation, vocation, vocation' and keeping a roof over our heads that the location, unless you are a gazillionaire is slightly less important.

So how do you really sell your home in today's real estate market? You have to have all the parts and pieces in place to make sure that it appeals to exactly the right buyer at the right time. You have to be willing to go above and beyond the call of duty in order to get it sold and mostly you have to be tenacious.

This book is for real estate agents that really do want to help their clients buy and sell in today's market, real estate investors who are looking to transact their properties in the shortest amount of time, utilizing the best exit strategy and securing the most amount of bottom line profit and most of all, for all the homeowners who <u>want to sell</u>, <u>need to sell</u> or <u>will be selling in the future</u>.

If you are looking for some real estate fairy dust that you can sprinkle on your home to make it sell without any work on your part, then I will tell you that you chose the wrong book.

However, if you are ready to sell, ready to put in a little elbow grease and hear what it really takes to get your home sold, and possibly be slightly offended with the cold hard 'tough love' truth in the process, then congratulations, you chose well!

C'mon, let's get that house sold!

*Currently, as of mid 2012, there is enough existing home inventory supply at the current sales pace for 6.6 months.

* 25% of all June 2012 sales were comprised of foreclosures and short sales

* Parts of the US are still experiencing days of market of over 250!

Chapter One
How to Create Love in Your Home

Why creating LOVE so important

Home staging has been around since the 1970s and has really caught on within the last 10 years, not only in the United States and Canada, but it's reaching other parts of the world at a rapid pace. As of the writing of this book, APSDmembers.com , my home staging training company, currently has followers in 14 countries. One of the reasons that home staging is so important is because it truly makes your home look and feel better and get your buyer to fall in love with the home. Marketing and Curb Appeal are a part of your staging and they should work together to created the desired result.

Generally speaking, people think their homes already look great because they're used to them or they've grown comfortable with what they've created in their home. The problem with that is it's specific for them. It's not necessarily catered to who the new homebuyer will be, which is what effective staging does. It helps the new home buyer to "overlook" the problem areas. Staging also creates the right 'feel' to the property which is how home buyers express their emotions when they tour a home.

They might say "Oh, this room has a great feel to it" or "This reminds me of the kitchen we had in Denver, we loved that kitchen." The best staged home will get the home buyer to fall in love with the home on the spot for how it looks and feels plus put in an offer and move in! It has been proven time and time again; **Love Sells!**

There is however a difference between regular staging and effective staging. True effective staging will actually make a home *feel* better as I just mentioned. You might say to yourself, "How do I know if this home feels good?" When people walk in the door, right away they won't say something like, "Oh I love the color of this carpet." What they'll say is, "Wow. This place really feels good," or, "You know what, I don't really like this place. Let's go." They're talking about how they feel and that's what effective staging should do for a home. Marketing attracts them, Curb Appeal gets them to stop and staging helps them fall in love with the home. These 3 components should not only make the home look better, but they should create the right feel for the home. We call this the **home selling triple gold**.

Next, the home selling triple gold needs to speak directly to right buyer. This is important because if you can define and then do marketing, curb appeal and staging for the right buyer from the very beginning, your home will sell substantially faster for more money.

So if a current home is occupied by an elderly couple, the actual neighborhood might be in transition and the new homebuyers consistently throughout the neighborhood are now young families.

If you are just looking at home staging, an effective home stager would come in, and you can do this as well, take a look around and say, "Okay, this home is no longer lived in by an elderly couple, now a mom, dad and three kids under the age of five reside here."

Home staging is important because it can literally transform the house from the current owner to the new buyer in a matter of a few hours and that's very, very important. Just the fact that it can be done so quickly and yields dramatic results is probably already getting you excited about the sale of your home or listing! The same results can be achieved with effective marketing and curb appeal techniques.

So, for instance, you might go to into a beautiful mid-century ranch home and find pink lace curtains, which may have worked really well in the '50s, but in today's world those curtains would be considered very, very specific to taste. There's nothing wrong with pink lace curtains but it is likely they are specific of taste to the person that occupied the home.

Today, we probably want to go ahead and remove those pink lace curtains and put up something a little more neutral, maybe linen sheers or even a nice roman shade if it is appropriate for the style of the home.

We have to be careful about anything in the house being too specific to taste, which again is why home staging is important. It's important to look around and ask, "Is that specific to my taste?" Maybe your spouse is a hunter and you have lots and lots of animal trophy heads throughout the house or in certain rooms. Those are specific to taste.

You really have to stop for a moment and determine if this décor appeals to everyone or if it is specific to you, your family, your spouse and does it need to be packaged up and ready to be moved prior to showing the home.

The same is true with curb appeal. If you have none, then you are giving your potential buyer no reason to 'slam on their brakes.' If you have pink flamingos, well those may get a few 'brake slammers' depending upon you area and buyer but for the most part, you might just get people to slam on their gas pedal instead of their brake! Make sure that your curb appeal literally pulls in the right buyer as well.

Finally your marketing. The funny thing about marketing is this is where most people get very generic but it is usually the first place prospects will experience your home. So take the time to define your buyer and speak directly to them in your marketing. If this home is horse property, your marketing should reflect that. If it is on a lake, I want to see the lake in your marketing. Define your buyer and refine your marketing!

Back to why home staging is so important, as we have said, it makes the home look better, creates the right feel to the home, speaks directly to the new homebuyer, makes the home seem less specific to taste and it differentiates your property compared to any other property. Let's face facts. A new homebuyer has their choice of a multitude of properties and they can, in a buyer's market, be very, very choosy.

They may look at 10, 20, 30, even 50 houses in today's world and choose anything they want within their price range. If your home is apples to apples in comparison to the other homes they're looking at, which for the most it is, the homebuyer will usually get very specific about location or a special feature of the area, neighborhood or home.

For example the homebuyer may want three bedrooms, three bathrooms, a two-car garage, a specific school district and want to be in the $300,000 price range. They're going to be looking at many houses that have three bedrooms, three bathrooms, in the right school district and similar price range. Effective home staging, curb appeal and marketing differentiates your property and makes it stand out in the buyer's memory from the other 25, 35 or 45 properties they'll be looking at.

The key to success is going for the gold with your Home Selling Triple Gold and making your property stand out above all the others.

 Hot Tips on getting every home buyer to fall in love with your house

1) Marketing Attracts the buyer, **cater to your buyer**
2) Curb Appeal gets them to stop, **create 'Brake-Stopping' Curb Appeal**
3) **Home Staging differentiates** your home from all the others they see and gets them to fall in love and buy the house

Staging with Love

Staging with love is knowing who your buyer is and speaking directly to them through your staging. It's really important to understand your buyer and know that every buyer is different. Especially in a buyer's market, we must speak to and appeal to that specific buyer. Otherwise, your house will never stand out and becomes part of a pool of homes that they're looking at. When you stage your home with love you really learn to speak to the heart, the mind and the spirit of the new homebuyer and their family. That's what staging with love is all about and I'm going to give you some very specific examples.

You want to give them staging scenes to become a part of, not just so they can imagine themselves living in the house, of course you want them to do that, but you literally want them to become a part of the scene as they're looking at the house. You want them to sit down and enjoy something and pick up a magazine that you earmarked to a specific article that would speak to that buyer, such as 'summer camps for kids.' You want them to lift up a fluffy towel with a rubber duck on it and have a good laugh. You want them to engage in a coffee and bagel scene that you've created in the kitchen.

By doing this, you're starting to capture their emotions and showering them with love. You are filling them up with wonderful warm feelings that speak directly to them, embrace them and pull them forward. It tells them that they want to be a part of the home.

You want to literally give them moments to remember, share and embrace. This is truly what staging with love is, taking the time to really define your buyer and giving them specific scenes they can participate in as they're looking at the house and then giving them moments to remember, share and embrace while they're experiencing these scenes.

 Hot Tips on getting every home buyer to fall in love with your house

1) Know your **buyer**
2) **Create Scenes** that engage the buyer
3) Deliver moments to **remember**

Why Stage with Love?

Well, now that we've talked about why staging is important and what staging with love actually is, why do you want to do it? To appeal to the buyer. Staging is Marketing and Staging with Love is REALLY GOOD Marketing. This is very, very important. You want to tug on their emotional home-buying heartstrings. It is absolutely vital that you make your home stand out above all the others that they will be seeing.

There are two types of markets: a buyer's market and a seller's market. If you're in a seller's market, guess what? You get to dictate all the rules, it's your game. If you're in a buyer's market, the buyer dictates all the rules. It's their game and they have lots and lots of choices. So if you truly want to sell in the shortest amount of time for the most amount of money, you must learn to stage with love and appeal directly to the right buyer.

If the buyers are looking at 25 other houses, all with similar qualities and within the same price range, how do they remember your house instead of the other 25? That's what staging with love will do. It will literally put your home into their heart and they will carry it with them. Even if they look at other homes, they'll always come back to yours. If you do something extra special in the house that speaks directly to each member of the family, it creates a memory. They can also draw on past memories and we'll talk more about that during our pocket of emotion portion of this book. When you stage with love you clearly define the new homebuyer.

Using the example of a young family with three children, you define a mom and dad in their late 30s, with children under the age of 10. You want to stage with enough love to appeal to mom, dad and to each child because each individual child is also a homebuyer. We all know that in today's world children have a great deal of power and influence in buying choices, vacations, cars and in homes.

So we need to appeal to every single member of the family with specific choices that allow each and every one of them to engage in the home buying process, enjoy it and to claim the rooms or the living areas as their own. You want every member of the family to fall in love with the house. It's one thing to have one family member voting for the house, but if you have a unanimous vote from all five, chances are you'll sell the home.

You also have to make it irresistible so they just can't get it out of their mind. It's like the candy bar at the checkout isle when you're waiting in line. You're looking at all your healthy vegetables and all the good food choices you made, but you just can't get the Snickers bar out of your mind because it's really well-positioned. That's what you have to do with your home when you stage it with love, make it so irresistible that they simply cannot get it out of their minds no matter how hard they try. So when you stage with love, you must speak to every single person in the family that will be making a buying choice.

Each family or buyer is in a specific moment in time. Study your buyer and your potential buyers, understand where they are at that moment, define it and set your stage accordingly. If you want to appeal to young families, it might be that they have one child and another one on the way. A specific way to speak to them, to make the home irresistible, would to be to stage one room with love for a toddler, so there are activities and fun things to do for a toddler in that room. Then you would stage another room for a newborn.

This will tug at the heartstrings of the toddler, because chances are they have strong emotions about the baby that's coming, but it also impacts the parents in a big way. They can see themselves in the nursery. They pick things up, enjoy them and become part of the staging with love experience.

> **Hot Tips on getting every home buyer to fall in love with your house:**
>
> 1) Staging with Love is **REALLY GOOD marketing**
> 2) Stage for **each member** of the family
> 3) Make the home **irresistible**

6 Steps to Successfully Staging Your Home

It's one thing to talk about the effects of staging, why you can stage with love and what it means, but it's a whole other thing to actually be able to effectively stage your home in order to get it sold so we've created a six-step home staging pyramid.

At my home staging training company, APSD®; The Association of Property Scene Designers, this 6 Step Home Staging Pyramid allows APSD® Certified Home Stagers throughout the world to know they can go into a home, effectively stage the home and yield specific results. There are six steps to the APSD® home staging pyramid that will help you create staging with love in your own home so you can also get extraordinary results.

The six steps are:

1. Define the customer.

2. CCTF. (Color, Continuity, Theme and Flow) We refer to these as the four cornerstones of APSD® home staging.

3. Foundation.

4. Anchor.

5. Create the scene.

6. Layer in the Pockets of Emotion®.

Define the Customer

      Let's go through these one by one. First of all, define your customer. Your customer is your buyer and your prospective buyer. We've talked about how important it is to stage specifically for them so they feel loved and feel engaged in each scene. So how do you get to know your customer or buyer?

Generally speaking, most staging is just a blank slate. People will come in with a little boilermaker template and they'll continually stage the same way without stopping to ask who's going to be buying their home. When you stop and truly define who your buyer is, you can stage much more effectively and get results, which is why you're reading this book. So the first thing you want to know is who your buyer is. Below you will find a list of typical categories that should act as a guideline to help you further define your buyer.

- A young family, first-time homebuyer. Maybe they are newlyweds or are about to be married. Childless or with a toddler and/or one on the way.

- A family with the parents in their 30's or 40's with 2-3 children and possibly one on the way.

- A young single executive, possibly only looking to be in the area for a few years

- Empty nesters that are downsizing or buying the home of their dreams

- A single parent home

- Second home or vacation home buyers

- Upgrading to the next step

You have to stop and ask, "Who is buying my home? Who are these people? How old are they? How many people will live here? What's the makeup of my buyer? How do you do that? How do you find out who they are?

Look around the neighborhood. Walk through your neighborhood and determine who has bought homes in the last three years. If you're not familiar with who's bought homes in the last three years, then you can go to a title company or a real estate agent and ask them to help you in determining who purchased homes in your neighborhood within the last three years and what trends they can decipher from those purchases. You can even go to your local county planning office to determine what the plans will be over the next five years for this area. They will show you what has been slated thus far which will, in turn, give you a very strong indication as to who is moving into your neighborhood.

When you are ready to define your buyer, look at what surrounds the neighborhood. Is it an office complex or a downtown environment? If so, chances are you're going to have young up and coming executives in the area. Is it malls, grocery stores, schools and churches? Then you're probably talking about Middle Class. Take a look at the kinds of stores located there. Are they Nordstrom's and Saks Fifth Avenue? You're talking about a more affluent client and, generally speaking, affluence means they've been around a little bit longer. Of course this is a generalization, but chances are your buyers are going to be in their 40s, 50s or 60s.

To further research, take a look at the schools. What types of schools are in your neighborhood? Is it a nursery school? Is it a grade school? Is it a high school? By knowing the types of schools in the area now you know the age group of the kids of the families that will be moving in. Now take a look at the churches. What sort of churches are in your neighborhood? How many churches? This will tell you a great deal about buyer.

If there are several of one denomination it tells you about the beliefs of an entire community. If there are a wide variety of different types of churches this indicates an eclectic or possibly a multi ethnic community. How accessible are you to conveniences or are you in a remote area? Is your house on a lake? Perhaps it would be a second home. So take a look at your environment. Talk to a real estate agent, talk to other people in the neighborhood and ask them what trends they've seen. People like to live where they work, play and connect with others. Once you understand their needs and present your home accordingly, your sale will be a cakewalk!

The next thing to do once you determine who your buyer will be is to ask yourself, "What do they like?" You have to understand what they like in order to set the stage for selling, effectively. Let's use the example of the young family that we reviewed earlier. We have a mom and dad in their late 30s and three children under the age of 10. Chances are they're probably going to do a little bit of TV watching, game playing or have family movie nights.

You might want to think about staging with love using a big flat screen TV. This flat screen TV can be the existing TV of the family that's living there if the home is occupied, or it can be brought in by a home stager, or you can bring it in yourself as well. You can also use a resource called Box Props or Turbo Props and use a fake TV, that's absolutely fine as well. Sometimes this can even present itself as fun and intriguing. You can create a great scene with the TV, some movies and popcorn and stage a fun family night scene.

It is important to thoroughly understand what your family likes. Because they have three kids under the age of ten, they might like bicycles, sports equipment or great meals in the kitchen. You must determine who they are, what they do and what they like. Then, because you know who they are and what they like, you can stage with love and give them what they like.

What is important to them, what do they cherish? If their children are really important to them, which of course they are, then you want to speak directly to the children as well. Focus on what you can give to each of the children in their individual bedrooms and tie it in to an overall theme so the parents can enjoy the experience as well. Sometimes it can be about telling them of the activities in the neighborhood, the community and the schools. Or it might just be about the really amazing features of the home such as a pool, tree house and big backyard.

Look at other defining facts. What kind of car do they drive up in? Is it a big fancy car, if so they might be a bit of a car aficionado? You might have some kind of an emblem, photo, or logo item of a Mercedes, Jaguar or Lexus in the house to speak to this car buff and possibly more affluent client. There is no detail too small when it comes to clearly defining your buyer.

Are there pets in the family? If so, you will want to pay attention to that. If you live in a neighborhood where there are a great number of fences and pets in every yard, generally speaking, most people moving into that neighborhood will also be or will soon be pet owners.

People are very attached to their animals and one thing you can do in order to stage with love is to honor their appreciation and love for their pets and create a specific pet staging scene.

During one of our APSD® Certified Training Courses, I sent out an exercise in advance and asked them to bring it to the training. It was just a way to get our future home stagers to start flexing their creativity muscles. They each received a pair of reading glasses and were asked to define a scene based on the reading glasses. The scenes were awesome, creative and would certainly capture the attention of the home buyer but one scene really stuck out in my mind as it was such a great pet scene. Imagine, creating a pet scene with a pair of reading glasses!

One of our APSD® Certified Property Scene Designers in California, who is an awesome stager and designer created a bird watching scene. In it she included the pair of reading glasses sitting propped up on an open bird watching book, binoculars and a stuffed toy cat! It was hysterical and so creative.

Pets are important to their owners so always make room for the family's best friend!

Color

The second step in the APSD® six-step home staging pyramid is CCTF (Color, Continuity, Theme and Flow). This is the single most defining system that must be carried through each and every home staging in order to create the correct sense or feel for the property.

Effective home staging will yield the right feel, which is what will sell the home and that's what CCTF does. You have to have consistent color and a consistent theme that is carried throughout the entire home. Continuity will create flow and all four elements come together to create the right feel for the property. Color is often an enigma to people, but all you have to think about is having a color tone. You may have jewel tones or neutral tones, etc. Carry at least one color from room to room. Let me give you a quick example.

I love jewel tones, so I have a neutral foundation and then lots and lots of décor with jewel tones, emerald greens, garnet reds, topaz golds, beautiful sapphire blues and so on. It doesn't mean that I have to have all four colors in every single room in the house. What it means is that I should have at least one of those color tones in each room. Some rooms will have one, some will have two, others will have three, four or five, but at least one color must be carried from room to room to create the right flow.

Colors should work with the environment, so you wouldn't want to have beach colors if you're located in the tundra. Colors should also work with the décor and the overall theme of your home.

You can use color decks from Sherwin Williams, various other home stores and paint stores to determine the right colors for your environment. Make sure that you're paying attention to the color both inside the home and outside the home because light affects color and in turn color affects color.

Continuity

In terms of continuity, develop a theme that makes sense. When we talk about carrying through the color, we're developing a color theme that makes sense. You always want to make sure the color and theme are working together and are consistent. You don't want to have an Asian theme in one bedroom, a continental scene in another bedroom and then a farm feel to another. You want to be certain your color and décor theme is very consistent. The overall theme might be modern, classic or contemporary. You can stage with fun affects, but your theme must be consistent in order to create flow and the right feel.. The scenes have to be consistent in their presentation to the buyer, with the right scene for the right buyer. We wouldn't want to assume that the buyer is a young family and the décor and theme in the bedrooms don't matter. The right theme has to appeal to the right buyer.

Theme

The next step in CCTF is theme. First and foremost you never want to overdo a theme. If you are doing a French country theme make it very simple and tasteful.

Some people like roosters, so you might want to add a rooster but you don't want an entire barn yard! It would be the same if you're doing holiday décor. A little bit of Halloween decor can be fun, but you don't want people walking into spider webs every time they enter a room. Remember, don't overdo a theme, it is meant to add to the feel of the room and the overall house.

Keep in mind that a holiday is not a theme, it's an accent. Cows are not a theme, they're an accent. The theme of every home should make sense for the home, for the environment and for the buyer. So, again, the theme for every home should make sense for:

- The home,
- The environment, and
- The buyer.

Carry the home theme into the marketing as well and now you'll really connect your dots and have it make sense to the customer.

Flow

Flow works together with color, theme and continuity to give you the right feel for the property. We operate on feelings and emotions. When you walk through the property, it's very important that your buyer gets the right feelings.

They want to feel as though the rooms naturally flow into one another, they connect with one another, things transition easily and effortlessly in a natural pattern.

By the way, this is the job of a really good home stager. Not all home stagers understand how to create the right feel and the right flow. As a homeowner you probably feel it in your own home and now it is your job to create it for the next owner.

Foundation

The third step in the APSD® home staging pyramid is the foundation. It's the single item within a room that allows for a connection between the entire scene. Generally speaking, all items touch the foundation. So what are some foundations? It could be a large rug, a countertop, the base of a bathtub or anything that the other items in a scene are connected to. It used to be that if you walked into a living room and you had a big rug, people used to tell you to move the couch off the rug because it would make your room look bigger. The truth is, that also makes the room feel disjointed. Ultimately we're after making the room feel warm and inviting.

To bring a room together, all things must touch a foundation. That doesn't mean that the sofa has to sit on the rug with six inches of room left in the back. That may mean that one or two legs of the sofa touches the rug and connects to the rest of the scene. It depends upon the scene that you're trying to create, but every scene will have a foundation. Within your own house, if you're still living in it while it's for sale, you'll want to make sure that each room has a scene that connects with all the other pieces in the scene.

That's why we use a foundation, to give you a foundation to a scene in order to bring all those pieces together. I'll be showing you specific examples of scenes and how you can use them to create staging with love in your house in the photo portfolio.

As I mentioned before, a foundation connects the scene and brings all the components together. It carries the CCTF throughout each scene and then allows it to flow into the next room. You can use rugs, mats, flooring, murals, flowerbeds, etc. A foundation can be both inside the home and outside the home.

Anchor

The fourth step in the APSD® home staging six-step pyramid is the anchor. The anchor is one defining piece, fixed or otherwise that defines the room. It creates a focal point in the room. It might be a fireplace, a window seat, furniture or a view. Right outside my front window, I have a beautiful view of Pike's Peak. You might have a view of the ocean, a stream or a hiking trail. Any kind of a beautiful view can be the anchor.

Once you have an anchor, you don't have to worry so much about the rest of the house, although it should all still look good. If the house is empty, you don't necessarily have to stage all areas of the home. If it's occupied, as long as you put your main focus toward the anchor or the focal point in the room then the rest of it can also be staged, but doesn't have to have as much wow as the anchor.

The anchor area needs to be your wow factor in every single room. An anchor item literally centers on a scene, the focal point where your eye lands first in a room or where your eye is drawn when you walk into a room. It can be one large piece in the scene, fixed or otherwise. It can be a piece of furniture.

As I mentioned before, it might be a fireplace, bookshelves or French doors that lead out to an amazing patio or pool area. It might be a free-standing fountain. These are various types of anchors that you might utilize when staging your home.

Generally speaking, an anchor is where the eye falls first for the buyer. So walk into your front door as though you've never been in there before, walk in, close your eyes and when you open your eyes, where does your eye fall naturally? Now, if it falls on the big mess in the corner then you know you need to clean that mess up and try the exercise one more time. Generally speaking, your eye will land in your focal area in the home. If your home is vacant, you might only have to stage that particular area, depending upon the anchor. If the home is occupied, the anchor is where you want your wow factor to happen.

Scene

The next step in the APSD® pyramid is the scene. We've talked a lot about creating scenes for your buyer, so now let's talk precisely about a scene. A scene to me has three components. The **three components** are:

1. Where is it?
2. How does it feel?
3. Who belongs there?

You should always answer these three questions when setting up a scene: Where am I? In other words, what room is this? Does this room speak to me? Do I know what it's for? Do I know who uses this room? What happens here? How do I feel about this room? How do I feel when I enter this room and who belongs in this room? I equate this to my actor background in movies. When a movie begins, right away I ask, "Where am I? How do I feel? Is this a scary movie? Am I walking into the dark woods? How do I feel about that? Who are the characters? Who are the people that are brave enough to walk into this dark forest?"

Of course you don't want your house to look like a dark forest, but it is important that you always think about those three questions: Where am I? How do I feel? Who belongs here? If you can answer these three questions then you've done a really effective job of staging with love.

Pockets of Emotion®

Then the final step in the six-step APSD® home staging pyramid is Pockets of Emotion®. Pockets of Emotion® are the single defining moment that makes your customer pause, remember, enjoy, laugh and share. When correctly used, a Pockets of Emotion® is the single best selling tool in selling real estate. You can use one per room or one per house. A lot of times in the kid's room, Pockets of Emotion® can be plentiful, but they should always appeal to the senses. Ready? Three points:

1. Appeal to the senses,

2. Appeal to the emotion, and

3. Appeal to the memory (and they often tickle the funny bone.)

Pockets of Emotion® in a baby's room could be little, tiny, preemie diapers, little-bitty socks or mommy bear reading to baby bear. There are all kinds of Pockets of Emotion® that make us say, "Ooh and ah," "I love it," or "It's so cute." In a kitchen, it might be something funny like a big pot on top of the stove with some dry pasta and a little rubber chicken and a cookbook open to Chicken Soup. It could be something really funny that is so obvious it seems to bite you on the nose and makes you giggle like a bathtub filled with rubber ducks or something that helps you to remember and name the house. A Pockets of Emotion® could be something very memorable and touching. It might appeal to your senses and it's a sensory recall from years ago. It might appeal to your memory. Photos are great for appealing to the memory. If you were viewing a home with a stream, what would you think if you saw an old photo of a grandfather and young boy with fly rods, tackle boxes and a canoe standing at the edge of the lake? It would invoke fond memories for you when you used to go fishing with your dad or grandfather and it will do the same for the buyer.

There are two things to remember in terms of Pockets of Emotion®; Some real estate professionals will still tell you to depersonalize but that is no longer the case, today, you want to personalize. Think about it, we are nosy, we want to know who made this house a home. If this weren't the case do you think reality TV would be so big? We want to know little bit about the family and if there's not one living there then make one up. Tell a story about the family that should be living there. Personalize the home for the buyer and make it memorable with a Pockets of Emotion®.

You'll find specific examples of great scenes with Pockets of Emotions™ that really speak to your buyer in the photo portfolio but below are a few simple ideas you can put together in a matter of minutes. These work in all types of homes, in all areas and can work whether the home is vacant or occupied.

You can do simple scenes, such things that we call mimic scenes, such as a scene of a dad paying bills and the kid doing homework. For this you can have two pair of glasses, pens, pencils, etc. In an empty-nester home you can do the bird watching scene with a cat and a bird book and binoculars that we introduced earlier. There are all sorts of scenes you can do and we'll show you the difference in living with a scene in an occupied home versus doing a scene in an vacant home in the next chapter.

All scenes support a larger scene. In a kitchen scene you might have a dinner scene on the stove and then a coffee service in another area and then the entire kitchen is staged. Each scene works in support of the next scene to create the overall presentation of the room and ultimately the home.

In a vacant home, you might be able to define a true strong anchor in a room, stage a scene around that anchor and not have to do anything else in the room. In an occupied home, we already have a bed and a dresser in this room, so we need to be able to incorporate the scene within the bed and dresser. That just means that every scene you do is always part of a larger scene. Make sure that whether the home is vacant or occupied, you're always staging scenes in terms of being a small part of a larger scene.

POE's or Pockets of Emotion® are great. As I mentioned before, there are several you can do. I'll show you specific examples of POEs that work in every single type of home. They serve to create memory and fondness, they appeal to the senses and they also tickle the funny bone. This is what helps the buyer fall in love with the house and want to buy it.

Hot Tips on getting every home buyer to fall in love with your house

1) Follow the **6 Step Staging System** to achieve fast and proven results
2) No detail is too small when it comes to **speaking directly** to your future buyer
3) The right **Pocket of Emotion**® will sell your home every single time

Chapter Two
Selling in the Shortest Amount of Time for the Most Amount of Money

Your Buyer is Not You

First and foremost, you will want to define your buyer. We've discussed at length the importance of defining your buyer, so you want to make sure that you really embrace the fact that your buyer IS NOT you. One of the biggest mistakes that sellers make is that they assume that the buyer will be like them and very rarely in today's world is the buyer exactly like the seller. Think about why you're moving. Are you moving because the home is now too small for you and your family? Are you moving because all the kids have moved out so you want to move on to another home? If you are moving, it is likely you are going to go buy a different kind of house. So you, in turn, will not be like the new seller as they are also moving for a specific reason, nor will you be like your new buyer. Each transition yields a new reason for moving and a new type of buyer or seller to take the place of the previous one.

The new family that's moving in might have a reason for moving as well, but they may be the same reasons that you had for buying the house 7, 10 or 20 years ago. You really need to understand your buyer; you need to know who they are, what's important to them and how to find out that information.

Visit your local planning office, evaluate the type of stores in the area, the schools, the churches and walk through the neighborhood with your eyes wide open. If you're not aware of who else is moving into your neighborhood, it's time to find out.

I'm a big fan of knocking on the door with a plate of cookies and saying, "Hi, my name is Karen. I know you moved in here a short time ago and I'm really sorry we haven't met. What brings you to the neighborhood?" Find out about your neighbors if you don't already know them. Ask them very pointed questions:

- What brings you to the neighborhood?
- Tell me about your family?
- What attracted you to this street?
- What attracted you to this house?

That tells me a lot about what I need to do to make sure that I'm staging with love, that I'm honoring the new buyers enough to take the time to find out who they are, what's important to them and how I can fill the home with love for them.

The last time I did this the young lady who answered said her name was Emily and she and her husband were transferred there by the military. She was thrilled to be back in the neighborhood in which she grew up as her parents still lived there, just a few streets away.

She also has one of her favorite cousins nearby and she can walk her 5 year old to kindergarten. She was holding a one year old as we spoke.

This immediately told me a great deal about the 'new buyers' of the neighborhood. It told me that this was a family neighborhood, desirable to young families because it was within walking distance to a pre-school and a grade school. I also found out that it is a 'multi-generational' neighborhood. That means that I should be marketing to my neighbors! I will start by 'staging with love' for a young family with 2 children. One would be 6 or younger and a second would be 2 or younger, or even on the way. That tells me I want to have a fun and safe backyard with a sandbox or swing set. I also need 2 rooms staged for smaller kids. One should be a nursery and the second would be for a toddler or young child with games and safe toys to keep them engaged while others look.

Once the staging is complete, take photos, create a flyer and market it to your neighborhood. Let them know they can have their family 'right next door,' literally and you will be surprised at your results!

When it comes to actually selling or transacting your home, you have choices. You can sell the home in a variety of different ways. You can sell it on your own, which is referred to as a FSBO (For Sale by Owner). If you are marketing to your neighbors, this may work out really well for you and keep you from paying an abundance of transaction fees (although a good agent is worth their fees in gold if you need one). You can list your home with a real estate agent and they'll post it for you on the Multiple Listing Services system (MLS). You can even work with a real estate investor. There are the pros and cons of working with an agent, investor or selling your home yourself. Following, I will discuss each in order to help you make the best choice possible.

> **Hot Tips on getting every home buyer to fall in love with your house**
> 1) Ask your neighbors **pointed questions** to get the right answers
> 2) **Honor** your future home **buyer**
> 3) **Market directly** to the neighborhood

Working with a Real Estate Agent

Look for a good, active agent with a solid track record of sales, not just listings, although multiple listings are good as well. It shows they are well networked which could serve you well in getting a buyer quickly. This type of agent will work their tail off to ensure the sale of your home. The first step, once they have the listing is to place your home on the MLS in order to get it in front of other real estate agents across the city, county, and if needed, the country and the globe.

The kind of agent you want should have a strong network and when they post your listing on the MLS, they will then be able to direct other agents and buyers to the listing. The link to the listing can also be sent directly to agents and prospects in order to quickly increase its exposure. This is something you will want to inquire into upfront before signing a listing agreement. Ask your agent about their network of other agents as well as prospects. Find out how exactly they will use the MLS specifically to market your listing as opposed to simply using it as a 'holding' spot.

I would recommend that you work with a real estate agent that knows your area and specializes in your type of home. You can take a look at these items on the enclosed checklist (***See Appendix for Checklist and Resources.**)

Your agent should have a strong advertising connection with various media sources. A good agent will use not only signs and flyers, but will also have a good media connection with the local newspapers, big and small, and possibly with TV, as well as some Internet publications.

I have 2 agents that I work with often, on is with RE/Max and is always negotiating a new ad in the local paper, real estate catalogues and as many effective media outlets as possible. She has developed a relationship with the sales reps for all of these publications so they are happy to work with her on larger, more creative and featured ads. The other is with Keller Williams and is equally dynamic in her approach with media, buyers and sellers.

Your agent should be equally as good at online marketing. How will your home be featured online? Will it be posted on a company website, the agent's site, on social media, etc? Again, review the checklist* and make sure that your agent is your marketing machine!

Another big advantage of using a real estate agent is that most real estate offices have had their contracts done by a legal professional. Much of the contract is standard, because they have to follow certain laws, but they also have legal professionals on staff or access to legal professionals should there be an unusual situation that comes about. This is normally included in the real estate commission which is a big advantage.

If you were selling your home on your own and had to go to an attorney, you can expect to pay for their time, not only with the overall transaction but additionally should there be more extensive questions, research or paperwork.

The agent will also handle your showings, which can be good and bad depending upon the agent. Again, discuss with your agent exactly how they want the home to be presented and shown in order to make every showing a success. Don't guess, be specific about how the home should look, smell, what should be left out what should be put away, you should even discuss the pattern or flow of how the home will be shown. While this can be a bit tedious for the agent, a good agent will love your investment in getting the home sold quickly and doing what it takes to make this happen. This is your biggest investment, make sure you nurture it!

The cons, when it comes to working with some real estate agents, is that they are not strong marketers, they rely too heavily on a sign in the yard, maybe one ad in the paper and the MLS listing. You will notice I said 'some' agents because you will also find strong marketers, which is what you want. You want to make sure that you have a real estate agent that's very, very actively marketing and, again, refer to your checklist* for how to best work with your agent. The checklist* will tell you exactly the questions you need to ask in order to develop a win-win and profitable relationship with your agent.

Some agents will have a hard time getting out of the same old pattern and, unfortunately, what worked in the seller's market will not work under any circumstances in a buyer's market. You want to make sure that it's an agent that not only knows your area, but that they have a solid and current history of actively selling homes like yours, their average days on market and, specifically, how they're marketing.

You want an agent that's willing to actively market your property and willing to get out there in new ways. You want them to say, "Yes, I am willing and able to do what it takes to get your home sold in the shortest amount of time for the most amount of money." An agent does not get paid until they sell your home, so help them get paid. You want to make sure that the agent knows your area like the back of their hand and they actively have a list of people that they market to that want to live in your area. What's special about your area? You and your agent should both know. Is it a blue ribbon school district? Is it accessible to every highway within five minutes? Is it horse property? What's extra special about your property? Your agent should have a list of prospects, or know how to find one, seeking your type of home.

You also want to know your agent's specialty. Do they specialize in a bread and butter home? Do they specialize in a Middle Income home? Do they specialize in high-end multimillion dollar homes?

Once you have that information, refer to your checklist* on how you and your agent can successfully work together in order to get your home sold in the shortest amount of time for the most amount of money.

Hot Tips on getting every home buyer to fall in love with your house

1) Choose an agent that has a **strong network** of buyers, sellers and other agents
2) Find an agent that **specializes in your area** and your type of home
3) **Work with your agent**, not against them, to get your home sold

Working with a Real Estate Investor

Just like working with agents there are pro's and con's when it comes to working with a real estate investor. The checklist* on working with a real estate investor will help you to decide whether or not this path is right for you.

The pros of working with a real estate investor are that you can employ multiple exit strategies. You can do this with a real estate agent as well, but generally speaking, the agent will be a selling agent. A real estate agent will be more focused on the full transaction of the property vs. a Real Estate investor.

With a real estate investor, you have more options such as selling the home at retail or wholesale if you don't have the money or the inclination to fix it up. They might do a lease option, depending upon where you live and the laws in your area. They may be willing to do a rental or a rent to own on the property and manage it for you.

So you have what is referred to as multiple exit strategies, which are more commonly employed with an investor. Real estate investors tend to couple creativity with fast action. If you want to get out fast, working with an investor may be a good option for you.

There are some cons to working with a real estate investor as well. Sometimes they can back out. They often have a clause in their contract that allows them the right to back out, so you want to be aware of that. Also, you may not get any money until your house is sold. The same thing is true with an agent, but an investor may have the right to take a year or so to transact the property. It depends upon how you structure your contract with the agent or with the real estate investor. What you need to know, though, is that you have options regardless of with whom you work.

There are a few things you should be very aware of that are on the checklist* for an investor. Investors can be wonderful. Sometimes they get a bad rap and the truth is there are just as many good investors out there as there are good real estate agents as there are good people, but you should always do your due diligence. For the real estate investor, you want to make sure they know your neighborhood and they know your type of home. Again, if you are considering multiple or creative exit strategies, you want to make sure the investor knows how to effectively market your property accordingly and, hopefully, they already have a following of people that may want to buy your house.

If it is being sold wholesale, chances are a good investor will already have a list of other investors who will be interested in a quick sale. You want to know what their track record is and, personally I would recommend you ask for and contact their referrals.

I'd want to know whether or not they're listed with The Better Business Bureau, that's not a make or break for me, it's just a nice bonus. If so, look them up and find out their rating. You'll need to know how you will receive feedback and when they anticipate the house transacting and how if they are not buying it outright. Make sure you refer to your checklist* if, in fact, you're going to be working with a real estate investor.

One more thing you should be aware of is if they have a contract I would highly recommend that before you sign anything, read the entire contract word for word. If they're pressuring you to sign it right then don't do it. Take the contract to an attorney, pay the $100 or $200 to have the attorney completely review it and then decide whether or not you want to sign the contract. Keep in mind you should take this contract to a real estate attorney.

If the attorney says the contract is not conventional, that doesn't mean it's not right for you, it just means it's not a conventional contract. Make sure you take it to a savvy real estate investor attorney or real estate attorney that can properly review the terms of the contract and explain them to you.

> **Hot Tips on getting every home buyer to fall in love with your house**
> 1) Use **multiple exit strategies** when selling your home
> 2) Great solution for fast transactions, but be **clear on the terms**
> 3) Pay to have a real estate investor attorney review and discuss your contract before signing or agreeing to any terms.

For Sale by Owner

This means that you are going to be the one responsible for selling the house. You get to keep more of the money or if you're upside down or you don't have a lot of equity it means that maybe you won't have to bring money to the closing table (or at least, less money) to get out of the house. You can show the house on your own terms.

So instead of having the real estate office contact you about a showing today at 1:00 o'clock and you go crazy because you left the house at 7:00 a.m. for work and you realize the dishes are in the sink and your dirty socks are on the floor and so on and so forth. Now, you can show the house when it is convenient for you. You can say you are available to show the house on Wednesdays and Fridays at 6:00 p.m. That's a huge benefit, you have more control over things.

The downside of it or the cons is that there's no one there to help you, so you have to be very aware of that. Make sure you're being safe and smart. I wouldn't show the home alone. I wouldn't keep valuables out. Chances are nothing will happen, but you want to be very, very careful. You can easily download a real estate contract right off the Internet at The Division of Real Estate or otherwise known as DORA. I would always recommend that you still have a real estate attorney do your closing and paperwork. Just to keep you on the safe side, still use a title company and follow the laws and regulations of your city, county and state.

 Hot Tips on getting every home buyer to fall in love with your house

1) Set **specific showing times** that work with your schedule and allow you to show your home in its best condition
2) Download **contracts** online at The Division of Real Estate or have them drawn up from a local real estate attorney
3) Always **follow the laws and regulations** of your city, county and state which can be found on your county website

Marketing to Market your home

Now, why do we talk about this in terms of selling in the shortest amount of time for the most amount of money? Because it's your home, your largest asset and your largest investment, so you need to make some very specific choices as to what works best for you in determining how you can quickly sell your home. Deciding upon who can help you sell best, the agent, the investor or if you're going to do a FSBO, this will really help you to transact faster and better and, hopefully, for the most amount of money. You have to make sure that you understand and take into consideration the pros and the cons of working either with an investor, an agent or selling on your own. Take all factors into consideration before listing or before just putting a sign in your yard.

Another thing to take into consideration in terms of getting your property up on the market is really deciding upon your goals. Most people don't take enough time to do this, but if you're pressured to sell then obviously your goals will be very different if you're not pressured to sell. Are you in a hurry to sell? Do you need to get out from underneath this house as soon as possible because you've already bought another house or you've already been transferred to another city or you have some kind of a distressed situation so you need to exit as fast as possible? Or, by next summer you would like to move to a warmer climate so you're going to put the house up for sale now knowing that you may have to accept some price reductions. Or, you may want to get the highest amount and are willing to wait for the best offer.

So you have to decide what your specific goals are in selling the property, because that will also then tell you who would be the right person to work with or, in the case of a FSBO, without. You might want to start out on your own, see how you do and then, if you have time and need help, you can contact an agent. You might be better off working with a real estate agent from the beginning that has a track record of getting the highest amount of money, but not necessarily in the shortest amount of time. So you really want to stop and take into consideration what your specific goals are and know exactly what your house is worth in today's market, not yesterday's market or tomorrow's market. You must be realistic. It's not about how much houses have been listed at, it's about how much they are selling at today. Then, based on those numbers, you can decide if you want to list a little higher, a little lower, if you want to stay on the market a little longer or if you need to get out yesterday.

In terms of marketing, many real estate investors and real estate agents will say they're already doing marketing for you, but the truth is that your largest investment is not their largest investment, so you want to make sure that your marketing is speaking directly to the right homebuyer.

Whether you're developing your marketing on your own because you have decided to do a FSBO or you're developing it with the agent or the investor, you want to make sure that you've stopped to define your customer effectively and then determine how to speak with love to the right buyer.

If your perfect buyer is a young family with three kids, they might have one child going into middle school, one in grade school and one still at home. In your marketing, especially when you are selling on your own, you want to speak with love directly to the parents and the kids, so your marketing might highlight the number one blue ribbon school district where your home is located.

It may showcase the bike trails, the community pool and the parks, all of which speak to the kids. Incentives are also a great way to capture the attention of the children which we will discuss in a later chapter. Your number one priority once you have defined your buyer is to speak directly to them with everything you do; marketing, staging, curb appeal, incentives…everything.

As you develop your marketing and your marketing plan, consider where you are going to place your marketing. Think about it. If you're advertising near the office buildings and business parks, but that's not where your buyer goes, then the message is not meeting the buyer. Make sure that your message is meeting them verbally and the text or theme is meeting them too.

When talking about the school districts, address the amenities that appeal to the kids and well as to the adults. If this is a home that sits near a lake, appeal to the fun and family time. **Message- Market- Match**. Make sure you message matches your market. And it reaches your buyer.

Last, but not least, once you've determined your goals and you're developing your marketing plan to appeal to the buyer, and you have chosen your selling partner, whether that's an agent, an investor, or whether it's you and your spouse and family, make sure that you connect the dots between your marketing, your goals and your partnerships so it all works together in one synergistic motion to ensure your successful vision of selling the home in the shortest amount of time for the most amount of money.

Hot Tips on getting every home buyer to fall in love with your house

1) Specifically **define your home selling goals** and priorities
2) Layout and implement a specific and **continuous marketing plan**
3) Make sure your **message matches your market**

Chapter Three
The Art of Prepping to Sell

Cleanliness is next to Selling-ness

The first thing you always want to do when getting ready to sell your house is to make sure the entire home is clean within an inch of its life. Clean every single part of the entire house. Most of the time, because we're used to living in our own dirt and with our own stuff, we don't realize that things aren't clean; we don't realize that we haven't cleaned light fixtures, baseboards or heating vents. We've just lived with it for so long that we don't see it. Go through the entire checklist* included with this book, on every single item that needs to be cleaned throughout your house prior to putting it on the market. This includes things that people can see but also things they can't see, especially in a buyer's market.

Stand in each room and take a look at every feature of the room;

Walls	Paint	Furniture
Ceilings	Curtains/Blinds	Decor
Lights	Curtain Rods	Vents
Light Fixtures	Flooring	Special Features
Switch Plates	Windows	Media
Baseboards	Window Sills	Plants

Look at each item and stand back and evaluate it. Ask yourself this question; If I saw this in a store would I love it or be put off by its dirt, color, condition or style? Depending upon your answer you will now know whether or not you need to address the items or areas.

Remember you are not trying to evaluate it based on taste, you or your buyers, but rather on whether or not it is appropriate for the selling goals you have for your home. If you are not sure whether or not you are being objective, find someone who is and brace yourself for tough love.

 Hot Tips on getting every home buyer to fall in love with your house
1) Clean your home like you are up for **the 'cleanest home of the year'** award
2) **Stand back and evaluate** all features and areas of the home
3) **Don't evaluate based on taste**

Utilities

Some of the things your buyer can't see are things like heating and air conditioning units. Get them cleaned, add new filters and have them certified prior to showing the house, as people will feel it, sense it, and see it. And, it will reflect well in your home inspection; the chances of an inspector bringing up an issue on a clean unit is very minimal.

On your checklist (***See Appendix for Checklist and Resources**) that I have included for you, take a look at all of those hidden items. These are the items that a very interested buyer will also want to inspect. The better they look, the less likely they are to raise concerns.

Appliances

Follow the same plan of action when it comes to cleaning your appliances. You need to go through and not just wipe off the front, the face or the handle, which of course should be wiped off anyway (yuk!), but go through the entire refrigerator and freezer. Pull everything out, wipe the whole thing down, including inside the door, the icemaker, pull out the produce drawers, wash those and wash underneath. It should look like a brand new appliance. If it doesn't have that 'Lowe's showroom' feeling, then keep cleaning! Make sure you turn your cleaner on in your self-cleaning oven and if it's not self-cleaning, use Easy-Off or another oven cleaner. Turn it on, wipe the whole thing out. If you do this once really, really good and take two days to go through your entire house from top to bottom or hire someone to do this, then all you'll ever have to do every time you have a showing is a quick 15-minute cleanup. Again, make sure you clean everything people don't necessarily see right away such as the heating units, appliances, etc. Maybe they did not notice it the first time but I guarantee you that they could 'feel' it. Unless you are selling wholesale, make sure your home feels as good as it looks!

Even today, I use a checklist* when I am preparing a home for sale or transaction. It is just that important.

Windows

Windows should be cleaned both inside and outside. I would recommend that you use a professional window cleaner to do the windows for you or use a more industrial product like Binswanger Glass cleaner. Make sure the windows are completely dry and that there aren't any streaks. A quick tip on washing windows, (my dad taught me this trick and if you saw his home where you could literally eat off the garage floor, you would know it is a great tip); it's best not to wash an outside window in direct sunlight, because the direct sunlight will dry the solution too quickly and it will streak.

When you wash a widow, wash the inside and outside, wash all the way around, so the trim, the sill, and the entire area is clean. Make sure you pay special attention to the glass in the corners. By the window latch and the lock, you'll have fingerprints or there'll be a little bit of grime, because over the years that's built up.

Make sure you take a good cleaning solution and get that whole area clean. Generally, soap and water and a little elbow grease will do the trick. I am also a BIG fan of the Mr. Clean pads but use them with gloves as they are very strong and will remove paint if you use them too aggressively! (and they are heck on your nails without gloves!)

The other thing to look at are your window screens. We all love window screens because we like to open our windows and get the fresh air, but the truth is, they look ugly and they make our windows look ugly, so I recommend, although some of you will argue with me on this, that you remove the window screens and put them in a nice stack in your garage and in your marketing material say that the home comes with a full set of window screens.

Many of you will laugh, but it's true. Your windows will look much nicer, from the inside and from the outside, if in fact you remove your window screens. So clean the windows thoroughly and remove the window screens!

Walls

You also want to look at your walls. Over the years, walls build up dirt and grime from people coming in and out, from the dog walking past and kids dragging their fingers. You'll be surprised, once you start looking at your walls, you'll see lots of dirt you never noticed that before. Yep, kind of gross when you really start looking, isn't it? Warm soap and water will almost always do the trick. If you need to have a little more scrubbing power, add a little baking soda to your water. If there is a lot of grime, again, I like Mr. Clean Pads, but don't forget those rubber gloves and test in a small concealed area first to make sure they are not removing paint or leaving a hint of discoloration on your walls.

Now here is the flip side of things…take an honest look at your walls. Do they need a good wash? Or, do they need a fresh coat of paint? A lot of times people will paint when they could have just washed. It is far more costly and time consuming to paint and you may be able to use that money and time in another area. While you're looking at your walls, let your eyes travel upward toward the ceiling because often we have all sorts of cobwebs and dust bunnies hanging from the ceiling, especially if you live in an older home where you might have an orange peel or popcorn ceiling. Take an especially close look in the corners of the ceiling and also around the light fixtures and beams on the ceiling. Simply run a soft mop around the corners and that will take care of your ceiling and crown molding. When I do staging consultations, both online and in homes, this is one of the areas that we always pay special attention to as a dirty wall or a spider climbing down to meet the buyers is a sure fire way to get them to turn tail and run!

Fireplace

If you have a wood burning fireplace or a pellet stove, more than likely you will have some smoke residue on the walls and ceiling. Simply follow the same advice as the walls by using soap and water or if appropriate, Mr. Clean pads or your favorite cleaning solution.

If you have smoke residue above the fireplace on brick you can either have an acid wash by a professional or try a foaming bathtub cleanser and a wire brush.

If your bricks are soft or in poor condition you will want to be extra careful not to cause damage. If all else fails, paint it! Go to your local paint store and ask them about the best type of paint to use for fireplace brick. You will be surprised at how this updates the look of your fireplace and makes the area much easier to clean.

Trim

When Pete, my husband and I married we decided to buy our first home. It was a beautiful home that sat at nearly 10,000 feet above sea level and overlooked the Rocky Mountains. The home stood empty for 2 years prior to us buying it so needless to say it was in need of a good cleaning. One day as I was cleaning all the baseboards and trim, Pete came in and asked me what I was doing. I said I'm cleaning the baseboards. He never realized baseboards needed cleaning! I told my dad this story, because as I have mentioned above, he is a cleaning fanatic, and he and I laughed for a half hour, with tears rolling down our cheeks, (Yes, I realize we both need to get out more!) about the fact that my husband didn't realize baseboards have to be cleaned! But, they are a perfect little shelf for dust so you have to make sure that you get all your baseboards clean. If you do this on a regular basis it simply means you can run a broom right across them and the dust will come off. If you haven't done it for a long time, you're going to need to get down on your hands and knees with a scrub brush and some soap and water, scrub it and then dry it. From there on out, you can just run a simple broom across them. I would recommend that if you are cleaning them yourself grab a gardening knee pad to use. Your knees will thank you later!

You'll also need to take a close look at the rest of the molding, such as crown molding, trim, etc. Especially molding around doors or areas that are common touch areas, you'll find as you look closely, there are fingerprints or dirt deposits lingering in the corners and crevices. These areas need a thorough cleaning or fresh paint.

Lighting

Then, of course, as you go throughout the rest of the property, you'll want to look at every single feature of the property. The next feature would be lights. Lights that are free-standing and lights fixed on the ceiling. For most of these, you will need to take down the globe or cover and wash it, get rid of the dead bugs, clean and polish the metal and remember to wipe off the blades of the ceiling fans. When you're looking at your lights don't forget about your switch plates. We touch these every time we go in and out of a room, so chances are every single one of them needs to be wiped down. Keep in mind that everything you touch, your buyer is going to be touching those things as well. And since we carry such a strong feeling of touch in our fingertips, we want them to carry a good and clean feeling with them as they enjoy the tour.

Doors

The same thing is true with all your doors, so take a close look at your doors. Give the doors a solid wipe down, front and back, paying special attention to the door knob area. Some of them may need a fresh coat of paint or a fresh coat of varnish.

The same thing is true with your door handles. Go ahead and error on the side of cleanliness and wipe the door handles down thoroughly. Door handles are one thing that your buyer will touch every single time. If you don't have nice, fresh, updated door handles, this is a place I would recommend you put some money into replacing (remember when I saved you money on washing the walls instead of painting them? Well, now you get to use that money!). Again, this is just a love connection between you and your buyer from the first moment they enter the home, because they're going to be grasping that door handle carrying that feeling with them as they walk through the house. It's one of the first moments of touch that they'll experience upon entering their future home.

Kitchen

Now, we've talked about all the basic areas, but as you go through the house take a close look at your kitchen. What do the appliances look like inside and out? If you are selling your house as a wholesale property due to its condition, you can paint your appliances. Again refer to a professional paint resource center and inquire into appliance paint. I would recommend you practice with this before using it on your appliances as it has a unique texture and sheen. If you are selling at full market value you need to make sure you appliances are in good, updated and clean condition. Some dishwashers have a front panel that slides out and turns over for another color choice. This is a great way to update your appliances as long as they are all still the same color.

Appliances should all match in color, but don't necessarily have to match in brand unless you have a high end home, then they should also match in brand.

Sink

Your sink is very important. Depending upon the style and type of home you have you can decide on what type of sink would go with the décor. If your home has a 'French country' feel to it, you can have a big, deep farm sink. If you have a more modern home style you can go for a copper sink. The important thing is that the sink goes with the rest of the kitchen and the sink. It does not matter what type of amazing sink you have if it is dirty, grimy and has old drain plugs that look like they were made from the tires of a junkyard Buick. Go buy a few new drain plugs at Home Depot or Lowe's and then really clean the rest of the sink so it shines! I like using a little soft scrub or baking soda and water in stainless steel sinks to really get them nice and shiny and then dry them thoroughly. Same thing with your countertops, if you have any countertop stains, use Softscrub. This also holds true with your smaller appliances, like toasters and coffee makers as well. If you want to stay green with your cleaning supplies, mix white vinegar, baking soda and water to create a powerful green cleaner. Love this!

Kitchen and Sink

A good rule of thumb to follow is 'metals match.' This is the same rule we follow in curb appeal, but it also holds true inside the home.

This does not mean they have to match entirely throughout the whole home but they should match within a room and within an extension from one room to another if both rooms are visually open to one another. So if your dining room is open to your kitchen the metals should be the same between the rooms but they may not necessarily be the same in the bedrooms. Having said that, your kitchen fixtures and hardware ideally would be the same metal. If you have a stainless steel kitchen sink then a nickel finish on your kitchen hardware (drawer pulls and cabinet knobs) and the same on your faucet and lighting fixtures would be ideal. These of course can vary greatly from home to home, region to region and trend to trend. An easy way to figure out what works best is to call on a certified APSD® Home Staging Professional, tour new open houses and pick up some current décor magazines like House Beautiful, Elle Decor and the HGTV magazine.

Cabinets

Next up are your cabinets. They need to be cleaned inside and out. If you have wood cabinets, I'd recommend that you clean them with Murphy's Soap and then give them a nice once over with some Murphy's Oil to really feed the wood and make it look healthy and shiny. If your cabinets have been painted or have a faux finish the best thing you can do is to wash them with soap and water and then dry thoroughly. Do this on the inside and outside of the cabinet.

Take a close look at your cabinets. If someone opened up the cabinet door would they find a complete disaster ready to fall out? Or would they find a nice orderly mixture of plates, mugs and bowls? You are striving for the latter! Remember your buyer is nosy so plan on the fact that they will open every door, drawer and closet!

Finally, if your cabinets need to be replaced, and they might in order to sell your home at fair market value, then get them replaced. Depending upon the type of home you have you might be able to go to Home Depot or Lowes. You may prefer to visit a design center that specializes in kitchens and cabinetry. Either way, consult with an expert in order to choose the best item for you home to get it sold quickly while reaping the profits from your investment. When I do home consultations cabinets are a focus point for us because they can literally make or break a kitchen. But there are several easy ways to update before you have to consider replacement.

Floor

Next is your kitchen floor. Some potential buyers will enter your home and out of courtesy or habit will kick their shoes off, so you want to make sure that they're walking on a nice clean surface. The last thing you want to happen is for them to look at the bottom of their freshly bleached white socks and see they have turned dull gray! We encourage this when I stage a home as it helps to keep the home clean but also makes the buyer think you are keeping the home clean for them!

A quick tip is to simply put a beautifully framed picture in the entry way that says "Kick off your shoes and stay awhile!" I think I saw that in the Martha Stewart Magazine, but if not, then it is still a great idea that I have used often for many of my home staging clients. Then add a small bench so they can sit down to remove their shoes along with several pair of rattan slippers in various sizes. The little blue bootie covers are for builders and workers, not for your buyers! The rattan slippers will give them a gentle massage with each step and even as they leave and put their own shoes back on they will continue to feel the massage which will remind them of your home!

If your floor is vinyl or laminate flooring, wash it with a wet mop and floor cleaner or dish soap. Then I like to use a spritz of Bona and a polishing mop. It helps to eliminate the streaks and gives your floor a nice shine! If you have a tile kitchen and you live in a cold environment, throw a small rug or runner in the kitchen so that they're walking on a clean warm surface versus a cold surface. You can find a wide assortment of kitchen rugs at Target and Bed, Bath and Beyond.

Bathrooms

As you move through the house, you want to take a look at every component of every room, the doors, the lights, the ceilings, the walls, the windows and the flooring. As you go through the bathroom, just like the kitchen, every single area should be sparkling clean. I'd highly recommend that you change your toilet seats as well as the bolt covers at the bottom of the toilet.

Get out your caulk gun if you have caulk around your bathtub, toilet or sink and give it a fresh thin clean coat of caulk in the color that matches the toilet, tub and sink, or clear. This will make everything look fresh as well as clean and many times they'll also think that it looks quite new.

Bathtub

Rub a dub dub…don't leave your tub looking as though there were 3 men in it! Think more along the lines of 'scrub a tub-tub.' Your bathtub should be completely free of mold, grime and icky stuff in the drain that shall remain nameless. You should only have 1 bottle of shampoo, one bottle of conditioner and 1 bottle of body wash. Put everything else under the sink until you need it.

If you have shower doors you might need to take a razor to the soap scum and Kaboom cleaner works very well too. Don't forget the door track! My favorite bathroom cleaner is actually a natural mixture of witch hazel, water and halved lemons. Let the lemons soak and then use them as scrubbers. They work wonders, smell great, and leave any white surface sparkling!

Should your bathroom contain a shower curtain, update the curtain, rings and rod upon the advice of your home staging expert. This is a quick and inexpensive way to update and refresh the entire room. At the very least change the curtain liner so if someone peeks behind the curtain, and they will, they see a fresh clean liner.

Hardware and Fixtures

Just as we mentioned in the kitchen all your metals in your bathroom should match. And unless you have thousands of extra dollars to throw around and your fixtures are solid gold, try to stay away from the gold tone in the bathroom. In general it becomes dull, flakes and is dated unless it is very expensive hardware.

Keep a package of Windex wipes under the sink in the bathroom for last minute showings. It is really easy to grab one, wipe down the mirror, door knob, faucet and tub fixtures giving you a quick clean in a flash!

Hot Tips on getting every home buyer to fall in love with your house

1) **Clean counts!**
2) Go green when you can with your **cleaning solutions**
3) **Metals match** within a room and within a line of sight

Updating the Home

Many of us have lived in our homes for a long time and have made our home what I refer to as 'specific to our taste.' Maybe you like valances or wall paper trim.

Perhaps you are a big fan of orange walls. Whatever the case, when you are ready to sell, it is time to appeal to the right buyer vs. hanging on to your specific tastes. And please don't fall into the trap of thinking your new buyer can 'imagine it' because, no, generally they can't and moreover, why would you want them to? There is too much competition out there for you to leave this up to the buyer's imagination so let's get it right the first time and get it sold!

It's time now to prep your property to sell in the shortest amount of time for the most amount of money, so we have to do what needs to be done to update the home. Before I go further, I know that someone is going to get mad at me. I know you think your home is beautiful and it is, because it is yours. But you are reading this book because you need to sell and that is what I am doing, helping you to sell. So when you move into your next home, by all means, make it specific to your taste again as that is how you turn a house into a home. But for now, please, trust me! This is a conversation I have with all of my home staging clients and my home stagers! I'm a big fan of less is more, so you want to be careful about not over fixing and not under fixing the property when you begin to update, refresh and counteract your original décor.

To figure out whether your home is a crowd pleaser or too specific to taste, look at other open houses and consult with your home staging professional. Make sure you are comparing apples to apples and then your home should look one step better.

You don't want to rock the whole house because you won't get your money back out of it unless the rest of the neighborhood has rocked their houses too, which still makes it an apples to apples comparison. If they all have new windows and you have old windows, unless you're willing to take the financial hit for that and the longer time on market (you'll get hit twice) then I recommend you just go ahead and get new windows.

First and foremost, keep in mind that most home sellers have created the home for them versus their customer. That's okay, you've been living in the home, but now it's time to cater to your customer. If you're trying to cater to yourself, you have to remember that you're going to spend foolishly and it will keep your property on the market far longer than is needed. Also, if you overdo it, it can be almost intimidating to the new homebuyer. Make sure that you're really defining your buyer and matching what you're going to be doing specifically for your buyer.

You never ever want to over fix the property and assume you can just charge more because of it. So if everybody else in your neighborhood has Corian countertops, it's okay for you to have Corian countertops. Then you'll stage with love, which is what makes your house standout above all the others. You don't have to get granite countertops. It should be apples to apples and then staged with love to differentiate your property from all the others. Now, the flipside is true as well. If you under fix the property, then you have to be prepared to also sit on the market longer and consistently lower your price until it sells at a wholesale price range. Don't under fix and don't over fix.

Hot Tips on getting every home buyer to fall in love with your house

1) Always make your **home apples to apples** with other like homes for sale
2) **Visit Open homes** or **consult an APSD® staging professional** to find out how your home compares to others for sale
3) **Don't over fix and don't under fix**

Current Trends

A few other things you want to look at in terms of updating, always keep in mind our philosophy of less is more in terms of décor, color, flooring, lighting, etc. Review current trends.

Do you have patterned wallpaper all over your house? Current trends may not show patterned wallpaper all over a house so you should probably remove the wallpaper. While new wallpaper can be amazing, if it has been up for 10 years or longer, I am almost certain it needs to come down! And yes, that includes borders. Ask yourself the question; 'What does my home look like in comparison to other homes that have been built in a similar price range and location as mine?" Based on your honest answer, you will know whether or not you have some updating in your near future, or if you need to price your home accordingly. In a buyer's market, you can't have it both ways. Either fix it right or lower the price.

So a few ways to find out what current trends are in terms of décor, colors, flooring, lighting, etc., is to simply visit newly-built homes in your area. Visit other existing homes that are for sale in your area as well. Look at magazines that showcase homes like yours. Go to open houses. Go to Home Depot or Lowes and talk to the designers on staff, there is no fee, they're there to help you and to give you answers, call me or consult a home staging professional. You may want to ask about the most common interior paint color. For example, "I live over in the Blue Fox neighborhood, what's the most common interior paint color that people are using in those homes right now? Our home ranges in the price between $350,000 and $375,000." They might say the most common color that they're seeing right now is Swoosh by Glidden or Peakcock by Behr. They may also say they are selling lots of cool grays or warm beiges. That is an easy way to determine current trends.

What if you love blood red on your walls but it is not a current trend or even a classic touch, what should you do? You should go ahead and neutralize that wall according to the direction and instruction of your home staging or design professional. You can always add some color with your staging and décor but a wall is viewed as 'unchangeable' so it is best to offer a neutral pallet. I know you are thinking 'well it is only paint, if I can change it so can they' but in today's world your home has to be as 'spot on' as possible in order to sell it in the shortest amount of time for the most amount of money. So many sellers are 'giving away the farm' when it comes to updates, repairs, closing costs and incentives. In order to compete, you have to make your home irresistible by putting it into the best condition possible and then staging with love!

You can easily and effortlessly update your home without spending hardly any money, simply by taking a look around at what's current, what's not, switching things around a little, using a little bit of elbow grease, maybe a can of paint or two and all this together really can make an amazing difference in your home. So if you're thinking about cleaning, clean it up from top to bottom. Thinking about updating? Take a look at current trends by comparison to what you have. Again, a little elbow grease, a little ingenuity and creativity can do wonders toward literally transforming your home. You may not even want to move after that! I also always recommend using a professionally certified APSD® Home Stager or give our office a call. While you can do this yourself, it is extremely helpful to have a professional come in, look at your home with a different set of eyes and offer their expertise and experience. And the best part is that a good home stager will cost you absolutely nothing because their services will pay for themselves when you are able to get your home under contract in half the time for more money!

Hot Tips on getting every home buyer to fall in love with your house

1) In a buyer's market, you can't have it both ways. **Either fix it right or lower the price**.
2) In order to compete, you have to **make your home irresistible** by putting it into the best condition possible and then staging with love!
3) **Consult a professional**

Organizing and Packing

Once again you can find a checklist (***See Appendix for Checklist and Resources**) that we've created for you in the back of the book, this time on Organizing and Packing. Organizing and packing can really make your move so much easier if, when you decide to stage with love, you also decide to pack with love. You can get very, very organized and prepared to move by simply getting ready in advance. So if you go through your house you may have all sorts of amazing artifacts that you've collected throughout your travels, photos, knickknacks, books and such.

I am sure they are absolutely gorgeous so you can leave out a dozen pieces and pack the rest so buyers can see that you have amazing bookshelves and lots of space. Buyers will enjoy looking at, sharing and talking about a few thoughtful mementos, but what you really want to do is begin packing most of them to avoid a cluttered look, remove a few precious and valuable items and get a head start on packing. And by the way, yes, it is okay to leave out a few personal photos and mementos. Remember, today, we 'do-personalize' as your buyer wants to know a little bit about the family that made this house a home. And, let's face facts there is no anonymity with Facebook, Google, reality TV, etc. So display a few personal items as it serves to pull at the buyer's heartstrings and builds a connection between your home and them.

Packing and organizing can be tedious. Good home stagers and professional organizers can help you with this. You don't have to do it all on your own, but either way, here are a few tips.

Go room by room because chances are in your new home you'll be putting things away room by room. I like to use those big Rubbermaid bins. You can color code them according to rooms. For example, all your bedrooms might be blue bins, your bathrooms are in green and your kitchen in purple. Next, I place a sticky note on the outside that tells me in which room it belongs and then exactly what's in there, not only an inventory list but a location notation as well and but depending upon whether I am going to unpack the bin or store it, I may also tape a Polaroid photo on the outside. For example, I might have a big Rubbermaid bin and with a sticky note that says 'living room' pasted on the outside. The next thing that I would have listed might be 'bookshelves' so it tells me the location of the items and third on the list would be an inventory of what's in that particular bin. Then the fourth thing would tell me what number this is. So if I need four containers, it might say one of four. Now whether I am storing, moving or unpacking I know exactly which room each bin belongs in, where it goes, what is in it and how many I have for that particular room or location. Easy to pack and easy to unpack.

As a side note, if you have packed something expensive, you may decide to also take a second photo for insurance purposes just in case it gets lost or damaged.

All of the labels get taped with packing tape on the side of the container under the handle so once they're stacked, I can easily see the label. I stack them accordingly in the storage unit or in a garage, depending upon how much there is to store.

Organizing and packing now, makes it so much easier for you when you are ready to move so you can see why it is like packing with love for yourself! Once you're prepared to leave, this makes selling and moving so much easier.

It might be that you have 1 of 1 or 1 of 20, but go ahead and organize it so that you know. When I took all of the items off of our bookshelves in our living room, it took me four containers so I had 1 of 4 in this particular category.

You can hire APSD® Certified Home Staging Professionals, you can hire organizers from NAPO, the National Association of Professional Organizers, you can hire a lot of people to help you do this or you can simply decide every single night you're going to clear out one area. It may not be perfect, but as long as you follow a system you'll then be able to backtrack and determine if you want to take more out of a room. Because you have a system, if you decide to add more packed items from any room, all you have to do now is simply adjust your box count. Instead of 1 of 4, you might have 1 of 5, because you decided you could clear out more.

Don't clear out so much that you can't stage with love. You can use your own items or you can rent items or you can hire someone who also has staging items. So you have three different options in order to stage with love. The important thing is that you understand how to do it. It's not important as to whether or not you do it or if you hire someone who understands how to do it. What is important is that it is effective and compelling and helps you to sell in the shortest amount of time for the most amount of money.

Now that you understand the system behind organizing and packing how do you actually determine which items to pack and which to leave in the home? Think about whether or not you've used them or touched them in the past 60 to 90 days. If the answer is no, then chances are you can pack them. If it comes to clothes, shoes or seasonal accessories, decide what you will use in the next 30-120 days. Keep those items out and pack the rest. If you live in a very remote area or there is something really unusual about your home that may make it more difficult to sell, you may decide to extend this through 180 days. Consult your real estate agent or selling partner regarding the expected days on market for your home.

Finally, I recommend that you try to avoid storing your containers in your garage, unless you have a very large garage. You don't want it to appear as though your garage is cluttered, too full or smaller than it actually is because it has so many extra items. You or your professional stager or organizer can rent a small storage unit to use while you are waiting on the sale of your home. And because you've already been very organized and systematic, it will be easy to arrange the unit according to the things that you anticipate needing first. So, you will pack the unit first with the items you will need the least. Your wedding china, that you've had for 21 years, even though you've never opened the box, you don't want to sell it or give it away, those containers can go in the storage unit first, all the way to the back. This will also protect them from falling or damage since they will be snug and protected. Then progressively categorize your belongings so when you need the items, they're more accessible to you.

If you have listed your home in February and you think you know approximately how long your house may be on the market, go ahead and pack your summer clothes and put them into the storage unit. Depending upon where you live, by April you may want to get to them if the house hasn't sold. Those items would be packed toward the front, or toward the door of the storage unit so you have easy access without unpacking your entire unit or PODS. This will put your mind at ease, and when the time is right, make your move much easier.

Hot Tips on getting every home buyer to fall in love with your house

1) Don't de-personalize, **do-personalize**
2) **Get organized** in advance so everything is easy to pack and **easy to unpack**
3) If you haven't used or enjoyed it for 90 days, **pack it**

Chapter Four
Staging with Love

Staging for Vacant Homes

Once the home has been properly prepped by cleaning, packing and organizing, it is time to stage. Whether you're staging a vacant property because you are moving or perhaps it is an investment property for you, regardless of the type of home, if the home is vacant you will still follow the same six-step home staging process that we have previously referred to as the 6 Step Home Staging Pyramid.

Start with defining the customer, next will be CCTF, then the foundation, the anchor, create the scenes and finally layer in the POE. The best part about the Pyramid is that no matter the type, location or style of home, the philosophy always remains the same it's only the items that change to align with the home, environment and buyer.

If you're staging a vacant home the nice thing is that many times you can create magic in a small space and you may not have to do the entire room. Other times you will have to do the entire room and it really depends upon the home, the space and the buyer as to what you will have to do. Remember, I have created an online photo portfolio for you to review so there will not be any guesswork and you can always call my office for a consultation as well, so don't worry, you can do it!

You might need to rent a bed and a dresser and then stage that part of the scene. It always depends upon the space, the client and the home. There are several rental companies that lend themselves to renting furniture but also renting specifically for staging such as American Family Rental, Aaron's or CORT. If you are using a stager, they will already have these connections, if not just pick up the phone and call and remember, everything is negotiable.

Most larger homes will need more furniture. If your home is quite small or the room is small you may not need any furniture at all, but you might have to use very creative and selective home staging techniques to complete the scene. Usually if you focus on 3 key rooms in terms of furniture, you don't have to do the entire home. You can stage a master suite, a kitchen and possibly a front room, again depending upon the home. By adding furniture to these 3 key rooms and really making an impact on your buyer, you can now simply add smaller scenes to the other rooms in the home and still make it memorable while filling the space.

There is also a technique called 'expanding 'a scene. A great example of this is in a baby bedroom where I'll use little foam puzzle pieces that you can spread out on the floor and kids love them. Letters or animals pop out of the center of the piece, giving you 2 pieces instead of just one. Instead of keeping it all in one very structured puzzle block, I'll take pieces out.

While you always want to make sure the pieces connect, one corner might be touching the other corner, but the piece has been removed from the entire square and now it's more un-puzzled, if you will.

It also has been staged to appear as though a child has been playing there. If there are letters in the puzzle, you might pop out 4 of the letters. Maybe you have the letters, H, Z, I, and O. You can take the H and I and place them together, propped up on a chair leg or window sill and spell 'hi' and then use the Z and O to expand the scene and make it look 'active' by simply placing them on top of the rest of the mat.

You can also expand a scene with pillows and throws. One of the APSD® standards and procedures that we use is called a 'Waterfall' where you can really connect a scene and expand it. A 'Waterfall' is defined as: 'used to create a minimum of 2 without a maximum of tiers of items that connect in CCTF and touch one another, tier by tier to create the waterfall effect.' You'll have three, four or five sequential pieces that create a flow or a connection, and they all touch which gives a greater sense of flow to the viewer.

So you might have a couch with a pillow on it in the corner, and then a throw touching the pillow. The throw may actually go over the side of the arm on the couch instead of over the back. Then at the bottom of the throw you might have another pillow and a book. So you've really expanded the scene by simply being a little more creative in what we've used.

> **Hot Tips on getting every home buyer to fall in love with your house**
>
> 1) In staging, the philosophy always remains the same **it's only the items that change** to align with the home, environment and buyer.
> 2) Give the **kids something to occupy themselves** while the parents tour the home
> 3) **Expand your scene** in order to fill the space

Occupied Homes

When you are staging an occupied home, the good news is you don't have to use quite so many things as when the home is vacant. If the home is occupied, all of a sudden you have a whole different scenario. One of the things you have to be really concerned with is how to live in a 'staged with love' occupied home. Now you'll have to stop and think about, how you can create the right scenes for the new homebuyer while still living in the home until it sells. First, think about everything you have learned thus far, and apply it. One of the greatest challenges faced by families is the home needs to be spotless in order to sell in the shortest amount of time for the most amount of money. That's steps number 1, clean, clean, clean. Is it true you home can still sell even if it is not super clean? Absolutely! But it will not sell in the shortest amount of time for the most amount of money.

It may sit on the market for an extra month or two, or three and sell for a few thousand less than you would like. So, if you combine that few thousand with the few thousand you will have to also spend on holding costs suddenly you have lost $5,000-$10,000 dollars when you could have just spent an extra 15 minutes a day keeping it looking great. I would get the entire family involved and give everyone a daily checklist (**See Appendix for Checklist and Resources**) (packing, beds, dishes, dog, etc), just like I have provided for you. I follow these same checklist*s each time I do staging consultations for clients. Everyday, they need to complete the checklist* before and after work or school. Ideally, this would take them about 5-10 minutes in the morning and in the evening once the home has been given an initial deep clean. The next thing to do is to give your family an incentive. If you know you can make an additional $5,000 by getting everyone to pitch in and do their part over the next 30 days, then what will they get for doing so? Would they like something for their new bedroom or a new bike for the trails by their new home? Give them a reason to help, hold everyone accountable and then get your home sold!

In addition to getting the home clean in preparation for your sale, you can also organize, pack, and update. Refer back to the information we discussed regarding packing and discuss needed updates with your agent, investor and home stager. Do the best you can with the scenes while still making your home livable for your family I will give you specific examples next.

You can create a great kitchen scene for the new home buyers that will get them to fall in love with your home without impeding your own lifestyle fairly easily. Here is a simple example; If you have done your homework, you may have discovered that the new home buyer is a family with small children. Perhaps you are now an empty nester but the people that are moving into your neighborhood are young families with kids because you happen to live in a Blue Ribbon School District. Maybe it's near the holidays so you decide to create a cookie baking scene. You remember baking cookies with your kids when they were young, don't you? Can you recall a special instance when you had such a good time that you created a forever memory? How did the cookies turn out? Did Santa look like Rudolph but you still told the kids how great they tasted? Well, guess what, by creating that scene you are going to appeal to the new home buyer in the same way. When they see this scene they will think about the fun they already have with their own kids or the fun they had with their parents when they were kids and now, how much they are looking forward to carrying on the tradition. Right away you are already appealing to them, making your home memorable and unforgettable to the new home buyers. So, what do you include in the scene? You might set out a couple of sugar cookies mixes, a rolling pin, a pastry mat and a cooking bowl to create a really cute cooking scene for the mom and kids. If you live in an affluent neighborhood, you can differentiate the scene by using organic ingredients to appeal to the buyer. The scene should however always be complete or it will just look like scattered items you forgot to put away. Again, you can find great scene pictures in the Photo Portfolio.

It's not practical to leave the scene out on a regular basis, so all you need to do is create the scene, understand exactly what it looks like, put it into a Rubbermaid container and slide it under the sink. I also like to take a quick photo of the scene with my phone once I have set it up so I can just refer to the photo when I need to reassemble the scene. This takes about 1 minute. This is what I refer to as my Perfect Showing consultation and it is what I show my clients in order for them to create the perfect scene. When you know you have a showing or you are going to be gone for a few days, pull out the container, set up the scene, put your 'everyday' items into the container, put it back under the sink and now your home is easily staged with lots of love while being livable. Then when you get home from work or get home from being gone for the weekend, you can put it away until you have another showing.

Sometimes you will have a surprise showing, so I always recommend that your home is as good as it can possibly be every day before you leave for work, because you just never know the day the perfect buyer walks in the door! That doesn't mean it has to be perfect, but as good as possible. Small storage bins work wonderfully, especially in the bathroom to put away toothpaste, hairbrushes and all kinds of personal items as well. You can literally put everything in a little Rubbermaid bin, put it under the sink every morning, take a wash cloth, wipe off the sink, throw it in the laundry, pull out the fresh washcloth from the storage bin and lay that out.

I'm big fan of having removable scenes in order to still make the house livable for every single person in the house. These are the very best ways that you can prep your house in order to show it and sell it for the most amount of money in the shortest amount of time.

Hot Tips on getting every home buyer to fall in love with your house

1) **Incentivize your family** to keep the home in 'show' condition
2) Create **removable scenes**, take a photo of them and put them away until you have a showing
3) **Invest in small containers** that you can hide

Chapter Five
Love at First Sight

Marketing and Preparing your home to create Love at First Sight

You've all heard the expression that you never get a second chance to make a first impression and the same is true with your home. So many people are willing to list or put their home up for sale prior to it being ready to sell. I never recommend this, because you're wasting your time and you're losing potential buyers for your home. When you are ready to list or sell your home, make sure your home is ready to be listed and sold.

How do you make sure you are ready to be listed and sold? Your first step is to simply decide. Once you are really ready, now you just follow the steps we have been talking about throughout the book already. Choose your selling partner, whether it is to be yourself, an investor or real estate agent. Make sure they are right for you and your home. Secondly, you want to work with your selling partner to ensure a great marketing plan. Your plan should clearly define your goals and duties as well as those of your selling partner.

I would also suggest that you track the timeline and results. Once your plan is in place, review your marketing and make sure it speaks to your defined buyer and is placed in areas that they will see often.

This is when 'Message-Market-Match' comes into play. Your message should match your market. The job of your marketing is to act as a home buyer attraction vehicle, so you want to make sure that the message you are delivering is well received by your prospect and in a media that they see, use or experience often. If you were listing a really great downtown loft in a newly revitalized area of town that is close to a University you may not choose to advertise your home in the AARP publication but rather in the University newsletter.

Again, it's about defining your buyer, speaking directly to the prospect and making sure that your message matches your customer's needs and desires and it's in a place where they'll see the message often. The first impression they get of your home is, of course, in the marketing, so does the marketing say what it needs to say? Also, how does the home look in the marketing? What do the photographs look like? A good real estate agent will understand the necessity of good photos and take the time to get the right photos instead of just accepting what they get with a 'point and shoot.' It's very important that the first photo that people see is the very best attribute of the home. This may be the gourmet kitchen, pool, or curb appeal.

We'll talk further about great curb appeal in Chapter Six when we create brake-stopping curb appeal, but the first photo, generally speaking is Curb Appeal, and the first piece of marketing that people need to see must capture their attention. So don't settle for second best when it comes to Curb Appeal, get ready to knock it out of the ballpark. Again, a good real estate agent, investor or home stager can help you with excellent curb appeal, photos and marketing.

Speaking of marketing, let's get back to it! In creating your flyers, you not only want a compelling headline that speaks to the customer, you also want a really 'sexy' photo of your house. There are two components: 1.) A compelling headline in all of the marketing. Most people are inclined to say 'for sale' or 'for rent'. Well hello, we already know that because we see it in the for sale section or the for rent section of the newspaper or we pulled the flyer off the for sale sign. So you don't need to say for sale, for rent or even 123 Main Street at the top of the flyer. Instead you need to say, "This is the only house in a blue ribbon school district under $200,000," or "Historic Home…Lincoln slept here" or "5 minutes to Beach." Your marketing has to be sexy with its very first approach and then, also, in its overall initial presentation.

Hot Tips on getting every home buyer to fall in love with your house

1) When you are ready to list or sell your home, make sure your **home is ready to be listed** and sold.
2) The job of your marketing is to act as a **home buyer attraction vehicle**
3) The **first photo** that people see is the very best attribute of the home

Curb Appeal

Initially, people see the outside before the inside which is why Curb Appeal is so important. Generally people think only in terms of landscaping when it comes to Curb Appeal, and while it certainly is a large part of what you need to do, it is not by any means, all that Curb Appeal encompasses. What about the marketing in your curb appeal attracts the buyer. What do your signs look like? What have you tied in between the theme of your marketing and the theme of your curb appeal? What does the exterior of your home look like?

The appearance of your curb appeal is your marketing. A great Curb Appeal photo will capture the hearts of many home buyers. But often, real estate agents, sellers and investors won't show the exterior of the home. Why? Because it doesn't look good. We already know that this is an old trick. If we can't see the outside, there must be something wrong with it. As the buyer, if I show up to what I think might be a beautiful home and from the outside it looks terrible, I will be angry with my agent for wasting my time, and unfortunately you will have lost a hot prospect. We must have new strategies that create love inside and outside your home. Make sure that the exterior of your home has extraordinary curb appeal and tie your marketing theme into the theme of the curb appeal.

Curb appeal doesn't have to be expensive. It doesn't have to be a whole redo of the entire exterior of your home. Curb appeal can simply be a fresh coat of paint. It can be a freshly-mowed lawn, some pretty planters at the front door and maybe a little welcome sign.

It doesn't have to be breathtaking multiple tiers of stacked stones or a brand new pond in the front yard. It doesn't have to be all that, but it should be as engaging, charming and inviting as possible. It should be clean, neat and orderly. It should look as though it's easily maintained and it can look like it has possibilities. In terms of curb appeal, clean and neat, appeals to and speaks directly to almost any retail buyer. And once you create that, you can use the photos in your marketing, mimic the same type of flowers you have in your yard with a graphic on your flyers and place a sandbox in the back yard for the kids and tell them in your marketing that you have a sandbox for the kids!

Hot Tips on getting every home buyer to fall in love with your house

1) **Curb appeal is marketing**
2) Don't use old tricks, employ **new strategies**
3) Tie your curb appeal theme into your **marketing theme**

The Scent Experience

The third most important impression is the front door. This too is part of your marketing. What does the front door look like? Is it a good experience for them? Is it clean? Is it attractive? In what condition is the door handle? We'll cover all those points more thoroughly in the next chapter, but the front door is your first opportunity to give the buyer an experience.

That is really what this is all about, the experience for you buyer. The right experience will lead to a sale. In adding to each experience, you might add one special extra touch right there at the front door. One of the things I really like to make sure that happens is some fresh fragrant flowers. I love putting a basket of lavender at the front door because it reminds me of very fond memories of my grandmother, her lavender plant and lavender sachets. You can do the same thing with any type of flower or fresh herb and now is another opportunity to tie this into your marketing. If you have a fresh basket of lavender at the front door, create small lavender sachets with the property address and agents phone number tied to the bag. Make sure each prospect gets a sachet and now they will remember the home. This is good and simple marketing. In terms of scents and we have already briefly covered this, the nice thing about something simple is that people get a subtle scent.

The sense of smell stays with them longer than any other sense they have so they carry that special thought with them throughout the home tour. Keep in mind this is not overpowering because it is on the ground, not in their face, and it will be a very quick experience. Sometimes they may not even necessarily notice the basket of lavender or lavender plant at the front door, but they carry the thought, the scent and the memory with them. So upon entering, their first impression is, "Wow, this feels really good," or "This just feels right," or "Don't you love this?" Sometimes they'll turn around and say, "Did you smell that? Do you remember my grandma's lavender sachets?" So right away, they'll already be making great memories in the home.

The best thing you could possibly do is make your home fragrance free. What I mean by that is to remove the inorganic scents from your home. Many people will be tempted to put fragrance enhancers everywhere, but today, the majority of people find those fragrances overpowering and they can offend anyone with allergies. People will want to spray air fresheners and the same thing happens. Someone like myself, who has bad allergies, would walk in and feel as though I couldn't even walk through the house; I'd have to turn around and walk back out.

The other thing that people like to do is light heavily-scented candles. During the holidays they'll have pumpkin, cinnamon, spruce or vanilla candles lit and the same thing happens. The scent is overpowering and many times instead of attracting people it offends people and they don't want to look through the rest of the house.

As a matter of fact when my husband and I were looking for a home in a quaint mountain town, I toured several homes before he arrived to narrow down our choices. Our agent pulled up to one house that was absolutely charming from the outside. It was nestled at the base of the mountain, surrounded by sunlit evergreens and had a wrap-around porch, which I love. From the description, it was exactly what we were looking for and in our price range. I was soooo excited. We walked in the back door which entered into the kitchen and the owner had left a very strong pumpkin pie scented candle burning in the kitchen which was also open to the dining room and living room. The fragrance was everywhere! I simply could not get past the kitchen.

Not only am I not fond of candles that are food scented, but my allergies ignited so fast I could not even get past the kitchen. I had to leave what should have been my dream home because of a scented candle.

This is a drastic example, but a true one. The sale of a home was lost because of this and it was my understanding that they needed to sell. Ultimately, if you are working with an agent or investor, they should tell you this, but if they don't make sure you take the responsibility to do everything you can to make you home incredibly sellable!

When there is such a strong scent it seems like you're covering something up. It might make people wonder what the house really smells like if there are 16 scented oil dispensers everywhere. If you like that kind of thing, I recommend that you only use fragrances that are labeled or named linen or ocean, rain, spearmint, or something along those lines so that it's very subtle and only use them in select areas. I don't recommend that they're all over the house. You might just have one in a bathroom or one in a kitchen. That is absolutely fine.

Organic fragrances are wonderful. What I mean by that are fresh fruit and herbs. They are perfect for a kitchen, bathroom, patio or deck. Other organic fragrances can be fresh flowers, pinecones, or fragrant wood in a fireplace, mudroom or a basement. You can also use fresh fruits, like a big bowl of oranges, lemons and limes. It not only looks visually appealing, but it smells wonderful. If you want to get a little extra scent out of them, take a small grater and grate the bottom of one of the pieces of fruit. Put it back in the bowl, of course with the bottom down so people can't see it, but then it really has a nice natural fragrance that will be very appealing.

If you have cigar or cigarette odor, pet odor, or any other type of odor that would be considered 'unfriendly' there are a few things you'll need to do. If it's a gentle odor a good cleaning may do the trick. You may have to get your walls and carpets professionally cleaned and steamed to remove the odor. Another thing you can try is charcoal briquettes, just like you use on the barbeque. They actually absorb odor, so you can get a big bag of charcoal briquettes, fill up a couple of big tin pans and put them in the affected areas. I'm not saying put them directly on your carpet, because the charcoal briquette will stain, but put it in a tin pan like you'd cook a turkey in and put those in affected areas.

If you really want to get a little extra bang for your buck, sprinkle that with some baking soda and then also sprinkle the carpet with baking soda. These naturally absorb odors and over time, will do a great job but they are not instant. There are also specific deodorizers that you can find in Target that will also absorb odors. They're not perfect, they take some time to work, but they will help, especially if the odor is very gentle. If the odor is really, really strong it will help to minimize it while you're trying to take care of it in other ways.

If the odor has gotten into your walls and a good washing does not do the trick, you will probably need to paint the walls with some kind of deodorizing paint like Kilz. And, I really hate to tell you this, but chances are you will probably have to rip up your carpet, replace your carpet pad, paint your floor with Kilz and then put in a new pad and new carpet.

I know this all is very extreme and, of course, it is your choice.

You can just let it smell and take the chance of your house sitting on the market for a long time and continually lowering your price or you can go ahead and take care of the problem, list it a little bit higher and sell a little bit faster. Either way, you have to be prepared to deal with the scents of the home. There are good scents, which are organic scents, fruits, fresh flowers, fresh herbs, etc. and there are bad scents. Too much of a good thing is never good.

Hot Tips on getting every home buyer to fall in love with your house

1) Add a **basket of fresh herbs** or flowers at your front door
2) Give the prospects a **'scented' parting gift** to establish their memory
3) The best scent is **'no scent.'**

First Impressions

One of the things that we all love to do, when we're walking into a home, is to 'see' ourselves walking in through the front door as though we're walking into our home. Whatever wall is directly across from the front door, I like to hang a nice mirror on that particular wall. That way the people that are coming in as a new potential homebuyer, the first person they see in the home is themselves.

This is definitely **staging with love**, because you're hoping that they love seeing themselves come in through the front door. Above the mirror you can do a stencil, a nice wall sticker or even a plaque that says welcome home. Right away people see themselves, their face and a welcome home sign; this creates a great first impression.

Keep in mind that in creating a first impression, we really want them to feel very, very good. This doesn't have to be big, ostentatious and in your face, but it should happen very sequentially so their experience constantly elevates.

If we think back to the new homebuyer family for example, I like to do what I refer to as a mimic scene. As they come in the front door, they might see a mimic scene of an adult coat and a pair of snow boots, if that is appropriate for your climate. If it's not, it might be a big beach towel, a pair of flip-flops and a beach tote. So it depends upon what's appropriate for your area, but let's say it's a coat, a hat, a pair of gloves and a pair of snow boots and then next to it would be a tiny little toddler-size as well, maybe a big pink fur coat, little leopard boots, something really cute and sassy. This is a mimic scene, a little girl mimicking the attire of the mother. You want that mimic scene because it puts love in the home. Right away people will say, "Oh, that's so cute. Look at that!" They're touching it, feeling it and enjoying it. They're part of the scene. Now they're enjoying their experience and they're only one foot into the house.

They've had a great experience outside the house and already they've had several extraordinary experiences coming into the home; they've actually created a memory already.

They've seen themselves entering their new home, they've seen the welcome home sign and they've seen the mimic scene. They've created little Pockets of Emotion® within their own heart and at this point the next impression is for them to see their home keys. You might have a mirror that has a little key rack on it. You might have a little dish at the front entry that's sitting on a small side table or a sofa table where the keys for this property are kept. You should have two keys on a key ring and the key tag should have the address on it. It should say welcome home, 123 Main Street or, obviously, whatever the address is.

Now, you don't really want those to be the keys to your home, but you want to give the idea for them to understand that these are the keys to their property. Keep multiple sets of these keys and add the marketing information for the house directly to the set of keys. It is a take away gift for them and creates a strong sense of remembrance.

So, all in all, we've experienced the marketing from the very first point of contact when it really speaks to the buyer. The next thing that we did, before we walked into the house, we saw the curb appeal. It might be extraordinary, it might be really simple, but either way it should speak directly to the customer. The third thing that happened was we had a good experience and started creating memories right at the front door.

As we walked in we immediately get the non-fragrant scent of the home or the pleasant fragrant scent that appeals to the sense of smell, which is something that will carry throughout the home.

The next thing that we experience is seeing ourselves walking into our new home, someone saying welcome home or seeing it visually above the mirror.

We see the small mimic scene which is always endearing. Another example of this if it is not in a kid friendly area might be for an empty-nest home. Display a woman's golf jacket and a man's really crazy, outlandish golf jacket, a little hat for him, a set of clubs or two different clubs, and some golf shoes for her. Mimic scenes can be done no matter what kind of home you have, but the idea is before people get more than a foot into the house they have multiple experiences to fall in love with the home.

Once they get to the mimic scene they should already be saying, "Oh, this is great!" Then the next thing they see are the keys to their home. So now you see why creating love at first sight is so important.

Hot Tips on getting every home buyer to fall in love with your house

1) Let your prospect be the **first person they 'see'** coming into the home
2) The right **'mimic' scene** will immediately create the perfect feeling of love
3) Take away gifts always create a strong **sense of remembrance**

Chapter Six
Let's Create Brake-Stopping Curb Appeal

Captivating Curb Appeal

Enhancing curb appeal on a property is among one of the most important aspects of staging with love. Why? Well, think about it. Who would want to enter a house that doesn't appeal to them from the outside? Why on earth would you ever go in if you don't even like the outside? Nobody wants to do that.

A property has to capture a perspective buyer's attention and ignite her curiosity to make her want to check out the inside of the house. If you don't create really sexy and compelling curb appeal, guess what? No matter how much love and effort you put toward the inside of your home, no one will ever see it. Enhancing curb appeal is among one of the most lucrative steps you can take in selling your home quickly for the most amount of money.

Curb appeal can involve things like painting the exterior, planting some herbs or flowers in the front yard, polishing doors and windows, putting a nice doormat at the front door, landscaping, lighting and new hardware. Sounds simple, but it has a massive impact. In fact, no staging can be complete without working on the curb appeal. You have to make sure that you're literally defining your curb appeal for the buyers, so we always go back to that first step of the APSD® home staging pyramid.

Step number one is define the buyer, and let your curb appeal should speak to them. If you have a home that's selling for empty-nesters, your curb appeal should look clean, neat, beautiful and easy to maintain, because they may not necessarily want to take care of a property with lots of details and upkeep. If you have a home that's being sold for a middle income family, you might have some nice flowerbeds and some areas for the kids.

Again, something that's not necessarily high maintenance but that looks nice that a family can enjoy. Then you also always want to make sure that you're creating a scene for the buyers to really, really enjoy and participate in, just like the interior scenes.

One of my favorite curb appeal scenes to create is with birdhouses. I go to a hobby store like Hobby Lobby or Michael's, get little feathered birds and hot glue their feet to the perch on the birdhouse. Then I might hot glue another one onto a tree limb or onto the corner of a birdbath. I love creating fun curb appeal, because people will pull up to the house and they'll look at the birdhouse and they say things like, "Sssshhh, do you see the bird?" They whisper to each other and watch the bird.

When they notice it's not moving they get out of the car and start creeping up toward the birdhouse. They're engaged, having fun, enjoying themselves and really partaking in the experience. Once they realize the birds aren't real they have a great laugh and they've already started to fall in love with the property.

Hot Tips on getting every home buyer to fall in love with your house

1) A **home must appeal from the outside in** order to get anyone on the inside
2) **Define the Curb Appeal** specifically for the right buyer
3) Create **fun and interactive curb appeal** scenes

37 Points of Curb Appeal

There are 37 different points to curb appeal and I've included that checklist* for you. Let's go through the 37 points of extraordinary brake-stopping curb appeal right now. I'll combine them into 7 steps and they are broken out into all 37 points on your checklist*.

Step #1: The first point is 'metals match.' What we mean by this is any metal that you see within your existing line of sight from where you're standing should match the other metals around it. So this might mean that if you're standing on the front porch, your front porch light, your yard light, door handles, doorknocker, doorbell, anywhere that you have metal from that line of sight should match the other metals that you can see.

Currently some of the most common types of metals are oil-rubbed bronze or variations of antique black. There are a lot of different kinds of metals and whether it's a brushed nickel, an oil-rubbed bronze, an antique black, or copper, all the metals should match.

The one metal that seems to be past its prime, as we mentioned when we talked about bathrooms, is gold or brass, so you probably want to avoid those unless you have an abundance of the color and can't afford to change it. For the most part, the other ones are all okay and will fit nicely into the overall look and feel of your home. It should be as updated as possible and, of course, be at least equal to or just one step above that of your neighbors. Mailboxes are the one thing that people always forget because it may not be within their immediate line of sight. Mailboxes can be so much fun but if they are metal, try to match it to your other metals. If not, then as long as it is in good condition and works well with the overall look and feel of the rest of your home, it will be fine.

Step #2: The second point of the 37 points to curb appeal is exterior paint color and paint condition. First and foremost, make sure that you have a current color trend. Again, you can go to a Home Depot, Lowe's or Sherwin Williams or any good paint store and ask them about current exterior colors for your home location and price range. You may want to discuss this with the designers or color specialists on staff as this is part of their area of expertise and their services are part of what the store offers you at no additional cost. When I am training our Certified APSD® Stagers, I always refer to these people as there 'free staff' because their services are so valuable. When you speak to them about the colors on your home, you might find that your color tone or color shade is just fine and if it is not, or you have had a penchant for a fuchsia home, change it.

Don't offer a paint incentive because it will slow down the sale of your home.

And remember, the buyer cannot imagine what 'cool sand' might look like once they have seen 'far out fuchsia.' But they will certainly be memorable!

Most of the time there are three colors on a home, the overall base color, which is the bigger part of the house, the trim color, which is the trim around your doors and windows and then the accent color, which might be the color of the front door, if it's painted, any window shutters or possibly a garage door. So you want to find out the specific color trends or classic color choice for your type of home and area and be certain your color is current and acceptable. If you decided years ago that you loved lavender in your 20's and now you're in 50's and your home is still lavender, chances are your house needs a new color.

Sometimes if you live in a harsh sun environment you'll find that the front of your house, where the sun hits the most, is slightly more faded but the rest is in really good condition. You can get the paint color-matched at your local paint store and paint only the front, which is called 'facing' the home. That's also perfectly acceptable as long as it now matches the rest of the home in color and condition. So once you have made certain you are using or have the right color, check the overall condition of the paint on the exterior of your home. Sometimes the paint condition is not good, in which case it needs to be repainted. Other times the house is just dirty and you might go ahead and power-wash it. If you are not sure, test it with the power-washer first. But the rule of thumb is if it is starting to flake or chip or is any shade of purple, it needs to be repainted.

Here's a **word of warning** on the power washing. Some power washers are very, very strong, so if you haven't used one before make sure that you stand back, turn it on at its lowest setting first and try it in a small discrete area. Sometimes they're so powerful that even with good, strong, fresh paint they will blow the paint off. It is best to start from a good distance away and on a very, very low setting. Many times a good power washing will give your house the look of a brand new fresh coat of paint. You'll want to make sure you power wash the trim, the garage door, the doors and so on, but again, very, very gently.

If the front door is painted, is the paint in good condition on the door? Is the color still contemporary or current? Has the paint faded? If the door is stained, take a look and make sure the stain is in good shape. Perhaps it needs to be sanded and re-stained. Take a good overall look at your garage door as well. Is it also in very good condition? Is it clean? Is it working? Does it have dents? If it has dents, believe it or not, some garage door companies will be able to repair the dent versus replace the garage door.

Next, you will want to pay close attention to the trim on your house. Sometimes the base color is perfectly fine and in good condition, but the trim needs to be sanded and repainted. Also, because color affects color, take a look at the base color of your home. Often, you can do an update by just repainting your trim. If your base color is a type of beige, but it has a little bit of a peach hue, which was common several years ago, you can paint a warmer color of trim around it for a big improvement. Take a color swatch or sample to a paint specialist at a local paint store and ask them to help you warm up your base color in comparison to your trim.

Step #3: Number three is the view of the inside of the home from the outside. This is really important; we always say make sure that the property looks good from the inside out and the outside in. So if we're standing outside on the curb, take a look and if the home has blinds you need to create a straight line of blinds all the way across the house. That means that all the blinds should be pulled to about mid level where your windows connect. Now, not all windows go up and down like that, but if they do they should be pulled about mid level and, hopefully, open. If you can't do that then have them all open, but pulled all the way down to the sill, just touching the sill. What's important is that the look is consistent. If not, it looks sloppy from the outside.

Curtains should be the same way. They should all be pulled open equal distance as the next set of curtains. So instead of closing them all, because you don't want to leave them closed as it will make the home seem closed off and dark, I always pull them so that a fourth of the window is covered by the curtain on either end. So you have half the window open in the middle.

Make sure your windowsills are uncluttered and free from dead bugs, dust or anything else that might get on your windowsill. I've seen homes with half full coffee mugs or near-dead plants on their windowsills. Make sure that your windowsills are clean and neat and don't have extra 'stuff' sitting on top of them as though they're a shelf.

Finally, it can be tempting to 'stage' your window sills with candles, which does look pretty…until the sun melts them and then you have a melted, stuck candle on your window sill that also possibly bled and stained the sill, wall and carpet.

This puts a serious damper on your curb appeal, so just leave the candles off the sills.

Next are window screens and storm doors. Remove all your window screens, so the buyer can get a clean and clear view of your windows. I've mentioned this previously but it is really important. Screens are a great asset to any home and everyone enjoys them as they allow a fresh breeze however, they tend to dull the look of the home. Once removed, place them in a tidy stack in your garage so that you can have a home that's sold with a 'full set of window screens.' Your windows should be clean on the inside and outside and streak free. No matter what type of home you have, it's very important that your windows are 100% clean and, again, overall, that the interior looks good from the exterior. Remember what my dad says about not cleaning your windows in direct sunlight as they will streak and the best cleaner is either white vinegar and water or a cleaner specific to cleaning windows.

Step #4: Number four is the front door. Now, we talked about this slightly with the paint condition, but we want to make sure that the overall condition of the front door is good. If it's an older front door and is very dated it might be time to replace it. If it has a big crack in the bottom, you'll want to replace that front door. Make sure the color is current, strong and vibrant, or beautiful, neutral or warm. Make sure the coat of paint or stain is even and, also, that the door is appropriate for the neighborhood and the home.

Be certain that you don't have the worst front door in the neighborhood. You may decide that you want to upgrade your front door to make a really good first impression.

When you upgrade your front door, talk to the designers about what's current. Just because they have a door in stock does not necessarily mean it's the most current and best choice for you.

Step#5: Number five is the yard and garden. Take a look at the overall yard, front, back, sides. Make sure the grass is mowed evenly and trimmed. Depending upon how much your grass grows and your climate, it will dictate how often you need to mow. In the summertime you probably need to make sure that it's freshly mowed and trimmed at least once a week. You'll also want to edge it along a flowerbed, a driveway and a sidewalk. Your trees, hedges and bushes should always be trimmed so they are neat and even. Everything should be in a nice clean configuration.

If you have trash that's located on the side of your house or the front of your house it needs to be removed and put inside the garage or, at the very minimum, in the backyard against the back of the house. Trash should never be visible from the front or the side of the house. I live in Colorado and if you leave your trash cans outside it is like feeding time at the zoo for the bears! Needless to say, all of our trash cans are neatly tucked inside our garage.

I love mailboxes, because they are one of the things that people first see when they pull into your home. Look and see if yours matches the other metals in your yard. If it's visually in line of sight with the other metals, then it should match. You may want to add something fun to the mailbox, if it works for the home and your defined buyer. This does not mean a themed mailbox, but you might want to add something fun like 'Smith Family Lives Here.' You may stencil 'No Bills, Please' depending on the neighborhood you live in.

Make sure it looks clean and neat and that it's not all banged up and looks like the sun has been shining on it for 30 years without a fresh coat of paint. Mailboxes can easily be fixed up with a fresh coat spray paint. I like to use Rust-Oleum spray paint. The hammered finish gives it a little more texture and interest and I use it for a variety of painting jobs including mailboxes, railing, door knobs and outdoor light fixtures.

Flower gardens have the ability to create an abundance of emotion. Last week, my husband Pete and I were driving into town and he quickly pulled our jeep to the side of the road and pointed to a beautiful array of vibrant and healthy name of flowers. They were part of the landscaping and curb appeal of a local small church. Pete was so taken with the flowers that he turned to me and said 'we should try this church sometime.' Beautiful flower displays can fill you with passion and compel you to want to be a part of the experience.

Flower beds, displays, potted flowers and hanging baskets also add color and dimension to the home. Place at least one big pot of plants or flowers next to the front door, possibly two if you have enough space without making the area crowded. Display flower pots on either side of the garage door as well, we call this 'book-ending.' If possible, you should have some kind of flower garden in the front of your house, maybe around the base of trees. If you can't physically dig into the ground, you can use small terracotta pots. Plant the flowers in pots and place those in a ring around a tree. This is charming and you can take them with you if you like, but it's also really engaging and unique, so it helps to differentiate your property from other properties.

Depending upon the time of year, sometimes it's easier to plant inside of a small pot than it is to actually plant in the ground. You can set the pots right into a mulched flowerbed. You don't even have to plant them in the flowerbed, but you can mulch a small area, use bricks, stones or landscaping timbers around it and then set the potted plants in there as well. A flower garden makes your house feel like the 'I own a home' dream and that's really what you're going after.

Now that your own yard looks good, it is time to check out the condition of your neighbor's yard. Some of you will have awesome neighbors that keep their yard in great condition (and they will be grateful that you have taken the time to spruce yours up!) and other times this will require a "you've been a great neighbor but…" tough love conversation with your neighbor. All you need say is, "Hey, we're trying to sell. I'd really appreciate if maybe you and I could spend half a day cleaning up your yard. Would that be okay with you?" You can even offer to pay to have someone come in and help them clean up their yard.

If their response is, no, no, no, then find out about possibly planting some tall shrubbery or putting in a tall fence between you and your neighbor's yard so that visually it's not a hindrance to someone purchasing your property.

Last, but not least once your yard looks great and the neighbor's yard is cleaned it is time to add a Pockets of Emotion®. We talked about birds and birdhouses at varying lengths in different trees throughout your yard.

LoveSellsBook.com
by Karen Schaefer

You can also add a small little bench and a reading scene on the bench itself. Or, you might want to add a coffee and donut scene. If, perhaps, you have a home that's sitting on a golf course maybe you have a little table and a small scene with bagels and coffee. There are lots of little scenes and POEs that you can add into the curb appeal that will take your client's breath away, or give them a good belly laugh and make them fall in love with your house. Remember the idea I gave you earlier about the birds and the birdbath? In one home I staged we created a nice landscaped scene with a small cement bench, a book on bird watching, a sun hat and binoculars. Next I added a bird bath under a few trees about 10 feet away. Around the rim of the bird bath, I hot glued a fake feathered bird that I picked up at the craft store. I did the same thing on the perch of one of the bird houses. I was inside when a car pulled past and then slowly came to a stop in front of the house. I could see the couple in the car talking and pointing at the bird bath and then slowly, the woman crept out of the car. She kept glancing back at the man waiting in the car and I finally understood what was happening. They thought the bird was real and were trying to sneak up on it to further check it out. Finally, she was close enough to reach out and gently touch it and when she did, she jumped back in surprise and started cracking up! She went back to the car and told the driver, and soon they were both laughing hysterically. Needless to say, at this point, I walked out of the house, they were having the time of their lives and of course, had already fallen in love with the home before they ever came inside. As you can see, by simply adding a little bit of 'Love' you will 'Sell.'

Step #6: Number six is a feature area, which can include a view, a sitting area, a play area, a pool or a hot tub, flowers and, of course, your POE™, as we've already discussed. So if you have a feature area that's a view, make sure that you take full advantage of the view. If you're sitting in the front yard and your view is the ocean, make sure there's a place for people to sit and enjoy the ocean view. You may want to have a small cocktail table and two Adirondack chairs, a big pitcher of lemonade with cocktail umbrellas, a couple beach towels and two pair of sunglasses. That would be a really wonderful scene to create that includes a POE™.

Perhaps your view is like mine and it is a view of the mountains. I have two big wooden rocking chairs with footstools, tables and a big lantern so we can sit, watch the mountain (no it doesn't go anywhere but it is still awesome to see!), enjoy the stars and get the best of all worlds. To stage it, I would drape two big wool blankets over the chairs, add big comfy pillows and some hot coco mix with marshmallows. Now you have a great scene with a POE™ that enhances the view while inviting your buyer to sit down, relax and enjoy one of the best selling features of the home.

If you have a space that you can use to turn into a sitting area, you can have a reflection bench, a hammock, Adirondack chairs or a small swing under a tree. There are all kinds of sitting areas that you and your buyer can enjoy. A play area is also a lot of fun. One of my favorite things to do for a play area is a sandbox.

You can get these very inexpensively at any kind of toy store or even at Target. You can also probably find them at a garage sale. Place a little sandbox in the far corner of a property. Many people don't want sand inside their homes and I don't blame them which is why I like to place these in the far corner of the back yard. Even if a bit comes into the home, it is not that big of a deal since it can be easily swept or vacuumed, but this minimizes the opportunity. With sandboxes, and this is magic, if a child goes outside to play, that means they're comfortable in the home. This now gives the parents time to enjoy the home because the kids are busy and safe. And trust me if the kids like it, the parents like it too. So I love doing sandboxes and I might have a few balls and toys there for them to play with as well. If you have a big backyard you can create a baseball diamond, add some plastic baseball bats, balls and gloves. You can set up a volley ball game, badminton or even croquet depending upon the home and your buyer. The important thing to remember is to create a full and complete scene and cater the scene to the specific buyer.

A pool and a hot tub, sauna or Jacuzzi area are really special areas for you to stage with love and they also add to your curb appeal. Anything on the outside of your home that gets people to fall in love with your home, versus any one else's home, is good curb appeal whether it is in the front, back or on the sides. You should really make sure that you stage this particular area with special love.

If your buyer is a family you can add a stack of beach towels, some fun flip-flops and beach toys. I like to blow up something really fun, like an alligator and throw it in the pool or hot tub so now you also have a Pockets of Emotion®.

For a young couple or just a couple in general, you could have some beach towels, a little wine and cheese and a few candles for a more romantic relaxing swim or a relaxing experience in the spa. I use fake food items for this from one of my favorite vendors, Just Dough It. I don't tend to do lots of bottles of wine and glasses because so many people do that so it is less memorable, but when it's appropriate it's absolutely fine.

Just make sure that you have plenty of greenery and fresh flowers around your pool or hot tub area because it makes your buyer feel as though this is a wonderful sort of beachy, tropical, spa-like or peaceful experience. You can enhance the experience with beach towels, terry cloth bathrobes, flip-flops, sunglasses, suntan lotion, books, some snacks and then some kind of fun blow-up, if it's appropriate. So you have all kinds of options to create great curb appeal with your pool or hot tub scene.

We talked a lot about flowers around the pool and flowers around the base of trees. You can do flowers in pots. You can do flowers in the ground. The important thing is that any time you have a specific area it should always be defined with flowers or greenery. So a specific area might mean around a pool. It might mean the four corners of a deck. It could be every other step as you descend to go down from the deck to the backyard. Anytime there's a defined area, showcase it with some type of flowers or greenery and then add at least one strong Pockets of Emotion® to your overall curb appeal.

Step 7: The final point on curb appeal is marketing and, again, this is on your checklist*. How many signs to do you have? Whether you're working with an agent, investor or selling yourself, one sign in your front yard, in a buyer's market will never do the trick.

You should have a sign in the front yard, a sign at the end of the street, a sign at the entrance to your subdivision and as many signs as you can. When we do an open house event, we try to have a minimum of 35 signs. If there are not enough areas for you to place your signs, ask your neighbors that sit on the corners if they mind if you place a sign in their yard. You can offer to pay them a small amount or bring them a plate of cookies to say thank you. Let them know you are trying to sell quickly at FMV (Fair Market Value) so it will help to benchmark pricing and DOM (Days on Market) for everyone in the neighborhood.

Since your home already has a themed décor take the time to tie that theme into your marketing. We've talked about that very extensively in terms of the overall feel of the home. What is the theme of the home and does your marketing share that same feel? So if you have a young executive first-time homebuyer, the theme of the home might be very, very contemporary and the theme of your marketing should reflect the same. A great example of this would be to do a fun and funky loft style home. You could use contemporary furniture and art, lots of black, white and stainless steel. Your marketing signs might be framed in stainless steel to capture their attention. Then on your flyers, maybe you will print them on pale grey paper instead of white in order to carry the cool and contemporary look and feel through from the loft to the marketing of the buyer.

I love using directional signs, the signs that have big arrows on them. That way people aren't just guessing where it is, but literally the signs point the way toward the house and they should be all the way up to the front of the house. How often have you followed this type of sign when there is a garage sale? Trust me they work!

Speaking of garage sales, I like holding them while I am doing an open house. You would be surprised by how many people who will come to a garage sale. They may not be your buyer but almost everyone knows someone who is looking for a home. Now you have a team of 'sellers' out there promoting your property! A crowd begets a crowd and sometimes it is just a numbers game so do everything you can to get people to your home!

Finally, you can also get people to help sponsor you during your marketing efforts. A local coffee shop might be willing to sponsor you and hand out flyers. In turn, they can place their ad on all your flyers and possibly offer a free cup of coffee. Maybe if you have friends that are in business in the local area ask them to help you as well. Present the benefit to them or their business vs. how it will help you and chances are you will end up with a 'sales team' all helping you to sell your home.

On that note, get as many people to market for you as you can, not only business sponsors and neighbors, but also various contractors, workers and people within the community. You can talk to people who put windows in homes and ask if they know of anybody who is getting new windows, looking to buy a new home or are updating their home because they're moving and would they please refer them to your house. You can tell the postman as well. Ask your neighbors who they know that they want to live next door. Their daughter and her family may be looking! There are all kinds of people that will be more than happy to send people in your direction once they see that you have staged and applied curb appeal, because they too will be falling in love with your home and happy to spread the word!

Hot Tips on getting every home buyer to fall in love with your house

1) Follow the **37 points to curb appeal** to create 'brake-stopping' and endearing curb appeal for every single buyer

2) **Elicit the help of your neighbors** and local businesses when it comes to selling your home. One good sale helps everyone!

3) A **crowd begets a crowd** and sometimes it is just a numbers game so do everything you can to get people to your home!

Chapter Seven
Staging the Kitchen with Love

Adding Love to the Kitchen

Once you have prepared your home for sale, it is time to start really staging. Throughout this book I have already given you great ideas and reasons for staging but now let's specifically go room by room. Remember you can find photo examples of all these ideas in the photo portfolio at **www.SimpleAppeal.com/PhotoPortfolio**.

A kitchen is one of the most important rooms in the house when it comes to selling a home, but the question is why? Well, the kitchen is truly the hub or the central part of every single home, no matter what type of home it is. Families, generally speaking, they take their meals there. Many times the kitchen also serves as a home office or a place for the kids to sit at the kitchen table and do homework.

Many times you'll find a mudroom, garage or back door is located off the kitchen, so people come in and out through the kitchen. If you have children it's where they bring friends because they all head to the kitchen to go eat. When you have a family discussion, you generally meet around the kitchen table. When you celebrate, you celebrate with meals and that's around the kitchen table.

The kitchen is really the central or the focal point of the entire home and you've certainly heard the saying that 'kitchens and bathrooms sell the home' and that is still true in most cases.

One of my favorite ways to stage a kitchen where there will be a young family moving in is to place local newspaper clippings on the refrigerator of little league teams, cheerleading squads and local marching bands. Then I circle a face and write 'way to go Ryan!' on the newspaper. I shared this idea with one of our APSD® Certified Professional Stagers and she did the same thing. Then when she held the open house event (at which there were a few hundred attendees and the home received 3 offers…yes, in this economy!) someone walked right up to the picture, pointed at one child and said 'That's my son!' They thought it was such a wonderful touch and it served to immediately create an instant and wonderful memory for this family in what could be their new home.

Define the Buyer

In order to effectively stage the kitchen, we always come full circle and define who the buyer is. A buyer, again, can be anyone: a single person, first-time homebuyers, a young family, middle age buyers with kids growing up or empty-nesters. It can be any kind of homebuyer at all, and because every home has a kitchen, it's really important that we define our customer and speak directly to them.

Who is the buyer? How are we speaking to the buyer in terms of the kitchen? If you have a buyer that is an empty-nester, your kitchen will be staged very differently than if you have a first-time homebuyer that doesn't have kids.

In terms of staging your kitchen with love, we must truly define what that means based on the buyer and the home. No matter what, the philosophy always remains the same, it is just the items that change. As soon as you're ready to stage your kitchen with love, you will simply to follow the six steps of the APSD® home staging pyramid, which is to define the customer, CCTF, foundations, anchors, scenes and POEs™.

If your home will remain occupied, these might be scenes that can be removed and replaced in order to maintain the livability of the home.

If you have a home that is in a entry-level neighborhood, you can do great really simple scenes on a kitchen table, a kitchen countertop and even on top of the refrigerator. I was doing a home in Las Vegas, NV one time and it had just been rehabbed by an investor. There was a grade school about 100 yards down the street and the home was older with an inexpensive rehab. The neighborhood was transitioning from middle aged owners with high school children to younger owners of entry level income with grade school children. The scene we created was absolutely memorable and I have included a photo of the scene in the photo portfolio.

I started by defining my buyer which I have just described. Then, because the home was very basic and neutral, I wanted to add some punches of color but not overpower this otherwise modest home. I purchased clear placemats that had blue, teal and espresso colored polka dots and placed two of them on the breakfast bar. I then placed two teal colored bowels, spoons, and juice glasses also on the placemat. The breakfast bar is serving as our anchor, the placemats are the foundation and the dishes create the scene.

The POE™ was a box of cheerios, turned over on its side with a few spilled out on the counter. This is a 'real world' scene which everyone loved! Because it was cute, charming, and spoke to the specific buyer, everyone fell in love with the home the moment they stepped in to the kitchen.

You could practically hear the buyers say 'now this looks like our house' and that was meant in a good way because prior to the staging the home sat on the market for more than 90 days and once it was staged it went under contract in 5 days.

If appropriate, you may need to create a more elegant scene that includes live plants,, china and figurines and that theme can be carried throughout the house as well. Perhaps you have collected Lladro figurines and you decide to use them in your staging. You might have one that accents a kitchen scene, another in the master bath and yet another in a guest bedroom. These may be on top of a counter or the centerpiece for a kitchen table. Just make sure that you complete the scene otherwise it just becomes random accessorizing. Completing the scene means that you don't just have a random plant, candle or towel but rather a scene that allows the buyer to engage. Again, please refer to the photo portfolio. And always carry the theme throughout the entire kitchen, just like you would do throughout any other room in the house as well.

Some of my most favorite scenes are coffee or tea scenes and this can be accomplished very easily by getting a nice tray and including a little coffeemaker or an espresso maker.

If you are staging for a nice entry level or middle-class home, you might use a Mr. Coffeemaker, some coffee packets or some Maxwell or Folgers coffee and a couple coffee mugs. If you have a more affluent home, you may find that you want to do an espresso maker, maybe a Keurig coffee maker with flavored coffee pods. You can even add some sugarcane stirrers. No matter the home, you need to add 6-8 tea towels to a kitchen and one or two of those will be designated to a coffee or tea scene.

For a home near a business triangle you can substitute stainless steel to-go mugs because, generally, you're talking to somebody that's on the run heading to the office.

If you're in more of an empty-nester environment, you might have a two-cup Mr. Coffeemaker and tea cups with saucers or coffee cups with saucers. You may also have some cookies on a plate as if it's an afternoon coffee clutch versus a morning coffee run. Add some creamer to this scene but in lieu of regular cream replace it with powdered creamer. The more specific you are once you have defined you buyer, the faster you will sell your home for the most amount of money.

Great Scenes

One of our APSD® Master home stager trainers, did a great scene with two coffee cups, a coffeemaker, some espresso beans and then this really cute owl and a message there from her husband that said, "To my little night owl. Don't work all night. Love, Eric." It was very cute and very endearing and a great scene for that kind of house. So you can do almost anything like that. Coffee scenes are wonderful in a house.

Another great tip in the kitchen and really for any room of the house, is to stage scenes in places that will sometimes surprise people. They might open a cabinet, because in today's world, as we keep saying, everybody is nosy and so you can create a scene inside the cabinet for them to enjoy. That may seem kind of pointless, what if they don't look? If you create a great scene inside of a cabinet, maybe a snack scene for the kids with Ding Dongs, Cheeto's and Sprite, you can let the corner of a napkin stick out of the edge of the cabinet so it entices someone to open up the cabinet and take a look.

If you do something great and you want your prospective buyers to see it, give them the opportunity to see it by letting a little piece of the napkin or a box top sort of hang out of the edge. Just make it look purposeful rather than sloppy.

The stove area is a great place to do a cooking scene. Cooking scenes can vary from house to house, again, depending upon the home and the buyer. Remember, the philosophy always remains the same, just follow the six steps, only the items change to fit the buyer and the home. I like doing a cooking scene that involves pasta because it is easy, colorful and can be used in almost any type of home. Put a recipe book on a recipe stand and open it to a pasta recipe. This is called **'connecting the staging dots.'**

Next, add a nice big pot, and since dry pasta doesn't really attract mold, mice or anything else, I usually open the whole bag or box and carefully place it in the pot.

I might have one or two nice cooking utensils to go with it, some olive oil, sea salt and maybe a few spices sitting next to it. Definitely add a few tea towels or kitchen towels, because it adds warmth, color and depth and serves to soften the otherwise hard areas of the kitchen.

Then, in order to expand the scene, depending on if you are living in the home or not, fill a big colored colander with some red, yellow, orange and green bell peppers, whole carrots and some purple onions to give it a lot of color and appeal. Now you have this entire scene set up for your new homebuyer. It's not complicated, it's not hard and, as a matter of fact, if you want you can even have it for dinner too, but it's a great scene and easy to create.

So the tools of that scene are as follows:
- One large pot
- Two kitchen utensils such as a large wooden spoon and a pasta ladle
- Dried pasta, the more interesting the better
- A jar of spaghetti sauce or a can of diced tomatoes
- Olive oil
- Rock salt, sea salt or Kosher salt (you are really after a cool looking jar!)
- Various seasonings and if possible, fresh herbs such as rosemary and basil
- A medium to large sized colander

- Fresh or Faux vegetables to go into the colander (As a side note, don't try to make the vegetables look real if they're not real, just have fun with the scene).
- You'll also need a recipe book and a recipe stand
- And two hand towels, dish towels or two oven mitts.

So those are the components of a really good but simple cooking scene that you can use in every type of kitchen. Depending upon who your customer is or who your buyer is will determine what kind of pot you use, what sort of pasta you use, if you have organic olive oil or just regular olive oil and so on. And if you have a large space to cover like a kitchen island, you can add plates, napkins, utensils, placemats, place setting and any other logical kitchen item that would compliment this scene.

As you review the staging photo journal, you'll notice the different components of the various photos. With every photo you review, always start by defining your customer, then throughout the photo you will see the color, continuity, theme and flow that work within that particular scene. You'll notice that everything has a foundation and an anchor and then a full scene, along with, for the most part, a Pockets of Emotion®.™

A Pockets of Emotion® is not required every time. It shouldn't be in every single scene because you might have sensory overload, but it's important that you do incorporate them often enough that people really get a strong feeling for how wonderful the home is, how they feel engaged and connected in the home and that they absolutely have the opportunity to fall in love with your home.

So, once again, the steps on staging your kitchen with love is defining who your customer is and speaking directly to that person. So if the home has a family and there are two kids, one is in high school and one is in middle school, speak to the parents as well as to both of those kids, which means that mom might have left an afternoon snack out for them with a little note telling them what to eat and what not to eat, what time she'll be home, what time they start dinner, etc.

So speak directly to your buyer and make sure that your scenes are full scenes. If the home is occupied, you can simply remove the scene into a Rubbermaid container and put it underneath the sink, in a closet or behind the door while the home is being lived in and then display the scene when you know you have a showing. If the home is unoccupied or vacant, you can leave the scene on display.

If there's real food make sure it's only food that does not attract pests into the house. If it's faux food, don't try to pass it off as real food, but rather let it be decorative and fun. Every scene should be a well rounded and complete scene and in a few scenes you'll actually incorporate a wonderful Pockets of Emotion® in to allow your customers to really enjoy and experience the scene in its entirety.

Hot Tips on getting every home buyer to fall in love with your house

1) The kitchen, above all else, should always be staged as it is the **hub of every home**
2) Always **complete the scene** so you are not doing random accessorizing or as I like to call it, a 'drive by staging.'
3) Follow the **photos in the photo portfolio** to create the right scene in your kitchen

Chapter Eight
Staging Your Bedrooms with Love

Adding Love to the Bedrooms

There are multiple bedrooms in every home. Generally speaking, there's a master bedroom, which is meant to be for the parents, or owner of the home. There's usually at least one, two or three additional bedrooms, which are usually meant to be for kids or guests. Normally speaking, beyond that if there are more bedrooms in the house you have the ability, if you'd like, to use some of those extra bedrooms as home offices, craft rooms or home gyms. So you have a variety of options in the other bedrooms. For the purposes of this book, we're going to cover three main bedrooms with the option of a fourth bedroom. We'll talk about a master bedroom, a tweener or teenager bedroom, a toddler bedroom and then possibly using another bedroom as an bonus or office room.

It's important, again, to stop and determine who the person is in this room. Sounds like a broken record right? But the truth is, unless you define the buyer for the entire home and then room by room, you are missing out on the best opportunity you have to sell your home in half the time at full market value. Remember, with scenes, ask where are you, how do you feel and who belongs here? When someone enters a room in a house, they should know who the room belongs to and have a strong feeling while they're in that room as to why it's right for that person.

Master Bedroom

If the home is vacant, you may have a lot of empty space to cover. You have the option to rent or buy furniture and décor items or hire a certified home stager to use their own items to fill the space in the master bedroom. So you might rent a bed, possibly a dresser and two side tables, one on either side of the bed. If you do that, that's fine. If you don't want to rent furniture you can also use a blow-up mattress. The secret to this is to use two mattresses and then use six of those big Rubbermaid containers underneath the mattresses. Put the mattress on top of the bins and then put the bed skirt or the dust ruffle over the first mattress. Then put your second mattress on top and add a full set of sheets. I usually like to recommend if you're using blow-up mattresses, use at least two duvets to give the bed some softness.

I prefer the blow up mattresses that come with a stand, but obviously you can also use them in the way I just described. You'll want a minimum of four pillows. If it's a king-size bed use king-size pillows. If it's not, you can use regular-size pillows, but a minimum of four pillows and at least three decorative pillows. This is a room that you really want to feel good, special and inviting, so I always like lots and lots of fluffiness in this room.

If the house is vacant and small, you may not need any furniture at all. You can create what I refer to as a 'picnic setting' where you'll use a nice rug and a really pretty throw that you'll drape into the setting. You might have a few pillows and a tray that has two coffee mugs and some parenting magazines, school calendars or work files.

So if it's a small home, especially a starter home, you could get away with a simple picnic setting. A larger home often requires at least some furniture in order to adequately fill the space.

If it's occupied and you're going to be using your own furniture, make sure that your bedding is current, looks fresh, clean and new. If not, treat yourself to a new bedding set that you can take with you when you go, so you can get one that you really like. I always recommend that you buy things in more neutral colors and patterns, because you can later dress it up with a different set of sheets and decorative pillows of a different color. Think in terms of taupe, white, crème, grey or even chocolate.

<u>Great Scenes</u>

On the bed itself, you can add a special scene. Take a small tray, a bud vase with a little flower, a tea cup and maybe a really nice tea bag and saucer and a Fashion Magazine. Then maybe you have a little note from a husband to a wife that says, "Happy Mother's Day, Sweetheart. Sleep in and enjoy, we love you." Now you have a great little Pockets of Emotion® within the scene. Remember the similar scene I described earlier? The Master bed faced a wall of windows which looked out onto a completely barren back yard.

It was nothing but dead trees, dirt and rock. The owner did not have it in their budget to do anything about the yard nor did they want window treatments so we had a huge challenge on our hands. So we created a similar scene as I mentioned above, with a tray, a bud vase and flower, and a Gardening magazine.

The gardening magazine was opened up to a beautiful backyard and we added a note that said 'Happy Birthday Honey. Thanks for waiting so long, this one is for you! Love, Bob.'

Immediately your buyer will fall in love with this room because of the special sentiment but also they convince themselves that they will be getting a new backyard too!

The specific items you would need to create this scene are as follows:

- A bed with sheets
- 2 Duvets
- 4 pillows
- 3 decorative or accent pillows
- 1 bed skirt
- A breakfast tray
- Bud vase and flower
- Coffee cup and saucer
- Gardening magazine with note

I always say 'when there is an elephant in the room, talk about the elephant.' In this case, the elephant was the terrible back yard so we had to address it. By giving your buyer something else to fall in love with, the 'elephant' becomes invisible.

This works for almost any kind of house. In our example above, you may decide to upgrade or downgrade the tray, the cup, the letter, the magazines, but that kind of scene will work in almost any kind of master bedroom that you have. Again, complete your scene.

A bed without a scene is just another bedroom. If the box spring shows, add a bed skirt or a dust ruffle. I mentioned earlier that I like to have at least two duvets or comforters; one pulled forward, one folded halfway back for a more luxurious look and feel, at least four pillows, and three decorative pillows.

On the nightstands in the Master Bedroom, I like to have a matching or coordinating set of lamps and then I'll add an additional Pockets of Emotion® on either tableside, making one very specific for a woman and one very specific for a man, if that's how we've defined our buyer. On the man's side we might have a Sports Illustrated Magazine and maybe a CD player. On the woman's side you could have a little pair of reading glasses and a good novel. If the couple is an executive couple we might have business files on either side with some reading glasses and pens.

Then, if you are staging with furniture, you probably still have a dresser. The top of the dresser is a foundation. So, once again, you can bring a full scene together on top of that foundation. Depending upon how big the dresser is, you might create a little travel scene. This would include an itinerary, a hotel confirmation and an e-ticket. You could also have a small display of photos with you, your spouse and your kids.

The bed is also a foundation. The bed may be your foundation and your anchor. Just so you know the difference, the anchor is where the eye falls first, the foundation is the component that brings all pieces of the scene together. In this instance, they may be the same piece, so always keep that in mind. Obviously, your tray is your scene, your little love note is your Pockets of Emotion®.

So we've combined all of these things to come together to create a full and complete scene.

> **Hot Tips on getting every home buyer to fall in love with your house**
>
> 1) When there is an **elephant in the room**, talk about the elephant
> 2) A bedroom set **without a scene** is just another bedroom
> 3) Any **scene appropriate scene** will sell the room

Tweener or Teenager's Room

A tweener room is for a child somewhere between 7 to 13 years old. Depending upon your area, this room may be for a Tweener or a Teenager. If you already have furniture in the room, then simply use the furniture in the room. If you don't have furniture, you can use a big beanbag chair or two smaller beanbag chairs, a rug and then some specific things that speak directly to the age group of the kids.

Music will speak to most kids. So I place a teen or tween magazine that's opened up to a page about a rock star or a music star. Then I have something lying out that looks like music to them, but they're not quite sure, such as CDs. It's a good laugh for the parents if we lay out a Walkman or a Discman and some tapes or CDs. The parents get a real kick out of that because the kids can't quite figure it out and they want to, but the parent thinks it is really funny.

Then use some text books, note books, back packs, and even some sports equipment as well. You can mix these things up to create fun and interactive scenes which is the name of the game.

At one home we staged with a Tweener room, I used several of the items I mentioned above and then found an old megaphone and movie camera. Next to it, I put a white board that said 'Watch out Steven Spielberg…I am coming!' You should have seen the reaction we received from that scene!

These are just a few ideas on things that you can use to create a scene within a tweener or teenagers room and once again, we're following the six-step pyramid. If there's furniture, obviously, the top of your bed can be a foundation; the bed itself is an anchor. If there's not a bed or a large piece of furniture left in the room, you can create a picnic scene in this room with a carpet, a few beanbag chairs and some books, magazines and even homework.

Tweeners and teenagers are such large-driving buying force that we want to make sure they have solid activities in the home, which is why I like to have the tweener magazines, and something for them to listen to, play with or watch. So I usually add a CD player, TV, Wii, computer or some other form of interaction. The iPods are just too small so we don't normally use those, but we do show pictures of them in opened magazines. We also leave notebooks or sketch pads or something like that that they can write in. We want them to be involved in some kind of activity so that their parents can look and enjoy the house while they can hang out and claim the room as their own.

The components of this scene are:

- Rug
- 2 Bean Bag Chairs
- Homework
- Pens, Paper
- Backpacks
- Music
- Megaphone
- Camera
- Note

 Hot Tips on getting every home buyer to fall in love with your house

1) Give the **child and parent both something to enjoy** in this room
2) Offer **multiple interactive** activities
3) Your **POE™ can appeal** to the parent and child

Younger Child's Room

I always think of a younger child in terms of two to five years old. In this kind of room, again, if it's occupied and you have furniture, you'll be using the furniture as your foundation, and your anchors, where you'll create your scenes. If there isn't furniture, you can use something very simple like a big foam puzzle mat or furry area rug.

Those work great to create a foundation. You can separate the puzzle pieces and just slightly have the edges touch in order to expand the scene or use the area rug as you foundation with the scene placed on top of it.

Once you have a puzzle mat or rug you can add something fun there. You can have one of the little open tents in which kids can play. I'm not talking about an official tent. We don't want any zippers or closures, just the small open tents that you can get at any kids store or in the kids department at Target. They look like castles or fire houses and you can fill them up with little balls and dolls so kids can go in and safely play. My favorite one so far was in the shape of a giraffe. It was so cute in the baby bedroom and the kids just fell in love with it. They never wanted to come out!

I have also painted a wall with chalk paint and then we give the kids white pieces of chalk to color on the wall. I attach the chalk with a string to the wall so they can't run all over the house with it. They'll stand there and color on the wall that's painted with chalk paint, which is very endearing, to most parents. We've given the kids an activity and that's also another Pockets of Emotion® because you really involved them, they've enjoyed it, they experienced it and they shared it.

Speaking of giving and experience, once they child has done their drawing, take a photo of it and text it to the parents with a special note saying 'Thanks for visiting 123 Main Street. It looks like this home gives Emily inspiration! Let me know when you are ready to move in!' They will love it and it will create a special instant memory.

The chalk wall paint is a great idea for activity and then you can create your little scene with your foam puzzle pieces and a couple of picture books. Another great and simple idea is to set up two little stuffed animals and have plastic tea cups so there's a tea party going on. You'd be amazed how many little kids will go in, sit and enjoy the tea party and make conversation with the stuffed animals while the parents feel safe and secure looking at the home. Again, just like the teenagers or the tweeners, you want to give them an activity that's safe, attractive, interactive and is very endearing to both them and to the parents.

The items you need to create this scene are as follows:

- Puzzle Mat with 12 squares
- Chalk Paint, chalk, string and hooks
- Picture books
- 2 Stuffed animals
- Small tea set

Hot Tips on getting every home buyer to fall in love with your house

1) One **can of chalk paint** goes a long way in keeping kids occupied
2) Market the **property to the parents** with a photo of their child enjoying the home
3) Go get yourself a **tea set!**

Fourth Bedroom

Depending upon who your buyer is, you may be able to take a little more liberty with this bedroom. A safe bet on a four-bedroom home is to turn the fourth bedroom into a home office. This can be easily accomplished with a small desk and chair, some books that talk about creating money or creating income, (something by Donald Trump or Warren Buffet are perfect), a coffee mug, pencils and pens in a holder and possibly even a day planner open to a specific date with some notes jotted in, circled, and then add a Pockets of Emotion® on one date by penciling in "Dinner with the Donald" or something along those lines. It's humorous. People will get a chuckle out of it.

It doesn't matter if it's a high-end home or a low-end home, either way people will enjoy a scene like that and it doesn't take a lot to create, so if it is appropriate for your home and your buyer, go ahead and set up an office scene.

If you're bringing in a desk or if you already have a desk or a small table, all of those things will work. That is, of course, your anchor. On top of that is your foundation. That's where you'll put your pencil cup, day planner, coffee mug and so forth. You might also have a pen and paper there so you can jot down a few notes or anything else. Add a chair if possible as you will find it used in order for the buyer to enjoy the scene and realize this will work as a home office for them.

As a final touch, a rug beneath the desk scene acts as a foundation for the entire scene and also serves to define the space within the scene.

If you have a larger table or desk, simply add a desk lamp to take up some additional space.. You can also add a home computer if you like. If you have one, great; if not, you can probably find an old one that does not work anymore at a garage sale for $1 or $2 or even at Goodwill.

You can go online and find faux electronics at BoxProps.com or TurboProps.com. You may also find a few other good staging items at these sites for other rooms in the house. Then go step by step, connect the staging dots and put together the scenes so they are complete and make sense.

How do you know if a scene works? When people walk in and say things like, "Oh, my gosh, you have to see this," or "Do you love this?" "I can't believe it," or "It's so funny," and they start laughing or they start to pause and maybe remember, cross their arms, think about it and shed a tear.

Once, I stenciled a saying in a room by the light switch that said "Make all your dreams come true." A woman walked into the room, paused, touched the light switch, looked at her husband misty-eyed and said, "Emma would just love this."

All those moments are called staging with love, so we helped her see the love in the room for her daughter. Stop and think about what you can do that will really create love for the next person and you know it works when they laugh, when they share and when it gives them pause; you know that what you're doing has worked.

The components of this scene are:

- 1 Desk or Table
- Table Lamp
- Rug
- Desk Chair
- Pencil cup and pencils
- Calendar/Day Planner with Note
- Coffee Mug

Hot Tips on getting every home buyer to fall in love with your house

1) Turn a **4th bedroom into a home office**
2) **Appeal to an entrepreneurial spirit** (an greed!)
3) Be flexible with this room **depending upon the buyer**

Chapter Nine
Staging Your Living Areas with Love

Adding Love to your Living Areas

Every home has a variety of living areas, whether it's a living room, a family room, a basement, a spare room, a library, or even a home theatre. And it's really important that you define your buyer, once again, in order to effectively stage each one of those rooms with love. Our primary living spaces are a family or a living room and then, also, a basement. If you have a living room, but no family room, I recommend that you stage your basement as a family room.

A living room can be a more formal environment. If the home is vacant, again, you have the option to bring in some furniture. If it's a living room, I recommend that you have some kind of settee or small sofa and possibly two chairs. The other items I'd recommend would be some kind of a rug and either a coffee table or foot stools. This is plenty to have in a vacant home.

If you don't have a settee, a two-person sofa or a love seat, you can just bring in the two chairs, the ottomans and the rug and you'll create a nice scene in your living room. You may want to add something with a little extra special touch, possibly some pretty lamps and maybe a coffee table book that's open to a picture of an exotic location. I would also add specific décor to the environment. So if you live in more of a sunny warm environment, you may have a big huge bowl of driftwood and seashells.

If you live in a colder environment, maybe you have a big bowl filled with pinecones and river rock. You want to add décor items that are very specific to the area.

If your home is already occupied, obviously with your sofa, chairs, coffee table and rugs, make sure that each and every item touches your foundation. So, once again, we go back to following the six steps. Your furniture will be your anchors, so chances are your sofa will be the overall anchor in the room. The area rug in the room will be your foundation. So the sofa should be pulled slightly in toward the rug so the front legs touch the rug. Depending upon how your room is laid out, you will probably have one nice chair on either side of the sofa facing toward one another, not facing the sofa.

If you have a big fireplace and the sofa is facing the fireplace, now you may choose to use one chair on either side of the fireplace facing the sofa. The rug will go in the center between the sofa and the chairs. If you can have some kind of an ottoman or coffee table in the middle, that works best. That's where you'll have your coffee table book and your décor that's specific to the area. That may mean, in an entry level home, you might have magazines instead of a coffee table book. So you don't ever have to change the philosophy, you only change the items up or down to suit your home and your buyer.

You understand that the main furniture in the living room will probably be your sofa with your sub pieces, such as your chairs, coffee table and ottoman, being sub anchors and all part of the scene.

You'll notice, we didn't do a specific Pockets of Emotion® in this room, but we did some emotional appeal with the coffee table book and décor that's specific to the area. So it doesn't always have to jump out and bite your nose, but it might be nice and subtle and inviting.

Great Scene

I always like to do something specific to the area, because people are there for a reason. So no matter what your area is, find something that speaks to the people that live in the area. One time in Farm County in the Midwest we found an old milk bottle carrier with six old glass milk bottles. That was the décor and it looked really, really wonderful next to the coffee table book that we had, which also featured farms throughout the Midwest. So you can find a lot of fun and specific décor no matter where you live, it doesn't have to necessarily be oceans or mountains.

The other room in the house that I think is important to stage with love is a family room or a large basement that serves as a family room. Again, just like the kitchen, this is a center or a hub of activity. Depending upon who your buyer is, you'll decide how you want to specifically stage that room. If your buyer is a family with kids, you might go down into the basement or into the family room, add a big rug so there's somewhere for them to hang out.

You could add several floor pillows or beanbag chairs. Lay out a big board game, checkers or Monopoly and put the game in play, meaning, you should have players that are already on the board and money that's dealt out if you're playing Monopoly.

You can do the Twister game, the Twister arrow should be pointing to a color and then take a couple pair of sneakers, small ones and big ones, and put them on different color spots on the Twister game. This makes for a really cute engaging and inviting scene that both parents and kids love. You may find that kids get active with these and that's fine, because they're a quick fix for you whether the home is vacant or occupied.

If you're going to do either of those game scenes, make sure you complete the scenes. Add a tray of snacks and some bags of chips. I would keep all these sealed, by the way, but maybe a half dozen single sized chip bags all in one big bowl. You can layer in a few packages of M&Ms and Skittles and add some soda. Again, be specific with everything you do such as adding the old coke bottles or 8 oz. sodas to create greater appeal. Just complete the scene.

If this room is not for kids but rather an as empty-nester couple, you can still do a game table, but this time it's a card table, or a poker table. Set up a specific card game in play such as black jack, spades or gin rummy.

These are great scenes, for empty-nester's families or just for an extra entertainment area. Again, you'll want to make sure the game is in motion. You might have poker chips, a big bowl of pretzels, some snacks and possibly some cocktail glasses on fun cocktail napkins and this can be another Pockets of Emotion® depending upon what your napkins say!

Go to a party store or nice home and kitchen store like Crate & Barrel or William-Sonoma, and pick up a set of their fun cocktail napkins. They can be an appropriate holiday theme décor or have a funny and cute saying. Then you can also add a glass and a swizzle stick inside each one. You've created a miniature scene for all four place settings at the game table very inexpensively.

All you need to create this scene is:

- A card or game table
- Deck of Cards
- Poker Chips
- Snacks
- Glasses and Swizzle Sticks
- Cocktail napkins
- Score Card

So these are two great ways that you can really create an amazing basement or family room scene. Again, the game table or the game is your focal point or your anchor, the floor, rug, the table top, those serve as your foundation and then the scene is created by all of the pieces and components that we've talked about. Always start off by defining your customer so you know exactly what to do for each scene. In this instance, how do you know the scene is working? You'll always know when your poker chips are moved or when there are more people playing the game than what you started initially.

You know the scene is working when people actively participate in the scene; you've truly accomplished staging with love in the living areas of your home.

 Hot Tips on getting every home buyer to fall in love with your house

1) Give the **living room a more formal setting**, make family rooms more casual
2) Soda's, cocktails, snacks and decorative napkins make a **perfect scene**
3) You know the scene is working when **people deal themselves in!**

Chapter Ten
Staging Your Bathrooms with Love

Adding love to your baths

Most homes have a minimum of two to three bathrooms. Each bathroom is for a specific person or persons, so we're continuing to follow the same method or system that we've done for every single room in the house. Bathrooms are no exception, you must decide which bathroom is for which person and then stage accordingly.

Whether the home is vacant or occupied doesn't make a great deal of difference since most items in a bathroom are fixed, with the exception of an occupied home bathroom getting a great deal more use. I would recommend that if you have an occupied home, keep one Tupperware container per bathroom filled with exactly what you need to set out every morning before you leave for work or right before a showing so that the bathroom always looks clean and fresh.

And of course, drop your everyday items into the container once you have emptied it. So you can just exchange the items easily and effortlessly as needed.

A dirty or messy bathroom can literally instantly lose the sale of your home, even though they might like everything else. I mean think about it, do you want to use a disgusting bathroom?

Yuk! Always make sure that you're keeping the scene clean, tidy and put away at all times so that as soon as you need it you can undo all the dirty towels and put out fresh towels along with the nice little pieces of home staging décor so that your client truly feels like they are loved when they walk into this bathroom.

Master Bathroom

Usually every home has a master bathroom; however, an older home may not. The master bathroom provides great opportunity for you to give some extra love in your staging. There are many, many anchors in a master bath. You might have a Jacuzzi or garden-style bath tub, you may have a two-piece sink or vanity. So there are a few different opportunities for you to use those points as focal points or anchors in the bathroom.

If you have a really amazing tub and shower, focus on that area first. If it's not so amazing, I'd take a look at the sink area and see if that looks better. Whichever of the two looks the best is the one that you will define as the anchor and add the wow factor. The other two you'll do more minimal staging so that they really enjoy the whole feel and experience, you keep their attention focused on the best feature of the room and so it does not feel crowded or overdone. If you're doing a wow factor on a bath tub and shower area, make sure you have lots and lots of towels. I like to have what I call a full set of towels. If it's a not-so-big bathroom, you can have two bath towels, two hand towels and two wash clothes. If it's a large bathroom, you should double that quantity.

Take a couple of towels and put them on a towel rack, then roll two more towels and put them in the corner of the bath tub or Jacuzzi spa so that it looks like we have kind of a spa effect. You can do either two or three and create a pyramid. If I have lots of towels I like to hang one over the side of the tub or the shower door so it pulls the look together.

Then with the hand towels, if there is another towel rack hang those on the towel rack. I also recommend that you lay one next to the sink. Next, roll the wash clothes and put two of them on top of the hand towel next to the sink and then two more on the top of the tank of the toilet. Then next to that I might set something small and simple, a box of tissue, a few candles, something really simple. In the bath tub itself, you have the opportunity to do something fun like big bath beads or bath salts. You can do a big scrub brush and an eye mask and create a whole little scene.

One of my favorite things to do is bring in something from a local area that people will recognize. So once I do all those rolled towels and maybe some fun bath beads, I might bring in a little box of chocolates from a local chocolatier; people know the chocolatier so it's kind of a fun thing to add. I might have a romance novel that's open halfway and face down so when you take a bath, you have a little romance novel. I always remember my mom taking a bath and reading a book. I guess with 4 kids, she needed the break! These are things that are fun and endearing, but not over the top so people always remember them. They think they're cute and it helps them remember that particular area

On the sink itself, you have the hand towel, the two rolled wash clothes and depending upon the sink area or the vanity, it will tell you what kind of décor you can have. You can do everything from a box of tissues to two plants, two candles or a little dish of nice bath accessories like beautiful lotions. You can do almost anything, but if I'm going to add a Pocket of Emotion and I haven't done the romance novel, I might do something in the bathroom that's gently sticking out from beneath the hand towel that's lying next to the sink. It might be two plane tickets to Cancun and with a note that says "Get your suntan lotion out, honey, happy anniversary."

So it's one of those hidden Pockets of Emotion® that we talked about, but people will lift up the towel, gently pull the tickets out and take a look at them. You can print off a faux ticket online so it's not that big of a deal, but it's a really great opportunity to add a little POE™.

You could even just do the hand towel with the two rolled towels, a bottle of suntan lotion in front of those towels and then pull the tickets and the note out from underneath the towels or substitute a postcard in place of the tickets. Again, this works for any type of home. It's only the items that will change, not the actual scene itself.

So those are some great ideas for a master bathroom and I have included some specific photos for you on the master bathroom in the Photo Portfolio.

To create this scene you will need:

- ➢ 2 Hand towels
- ➢ 2 Wash clothes
- ➢ Suntan Lotion
- ➢ A personalized note
- ➢ Fake plane tickets or a destination postcard

Hot Tips on getting every home buyer to fall in love with your house

1) **Focus on the area** that offers the greatest 'wow' factor first
2) **Add a fun POE™** such as a romance novel or plane tickets
3) You can't have too many **towels in a Master Bathroom**

Family/ Guest Bathroom

Every home has a family bathroom in the house. It may also be a guest bathroom. It may serve as both. If you have a bathroom that's specific to the kids, you can have a lot of fun there. However, if this bathroom must serve both purposes, such as kids and guests, you need to tone it down ever so slightly.

If the bathroom is just for little kids, you can do a whole rubber duck theme: a rubber duck mat, a rubber duck shower curtain, white fluffy towels, yellow toothbrushes and have a very, very cute and simple scene.

If you already have items like this that's just perfect, use those. Put away anything that has the everyday mundane look, such as crumpled up toothpaste rolls, ugly-looking hairbrushes or dirty hand towels. All that will be tossed into your little rubber bin and the nice things will come out every time you have the opportunity to showcase the home.

Again, you will need at least one full towel set. You can hang a towel on the towel rack. Hang another one over the corner of the bath tub. You can set a hand towel next to the sink, just like we did in the regular master bathroom. Put a cute little shower mat or a tub mat just outside the shower. Then if you're doing something with rubber ducks or flowers, you can add appropriately colored toothbrushes. I like adding a fresh tube of bubble gum toothpaste or Barbie Toothpaste and a Barbie Toothbrush. Really simple things that add a nice Pockets of Emotion® and even if you don't have them they're very affordable.

Your Pockets of Emotion® in this particular room can, itself, be the rubber duck or the Barbie toothbrushes, but you also have the opportunity to do something really specific. So you could float a rubber duck inside the sink, which would be funny, but it is better to float the ducks in the bath tub and pull the shower curtain closed. Don't float them in very much water because you don't want anything bad to happen, but you could float 25 rubber ducks in an inch of water. People pull back the curtain, they're surprised, they have fun and they love it. As a matter of fact, you don't have to use any water at all. If you want you can just face them all forward and put them into the bath tub itself. It's one of my favorite staging techniques that works in any kind of home, but it is specific to a children's bathroom.

So the other kind of bathrooms you might have would be a guest bathroom. This could be a very nice en-suite guest bathroom, which I would stage as though you were preparing for a guest. It doesn't have to be over the top. Again, I like to use local décor specific to your community or environment. You could have a bowl of seashells, a bowl of sand, some pinecones, acorns or anything specific to the area that will resonate with the buyer.

Using local décor in the guest bathroom makes the guest feel more at home in their environment. Always use a nice set of towels on the towel racks, one over the side of the bath tub, one, of course, next to the sink like we always do and then something small and specific on the top of the toilet tank as well. I usually like to have some kind of floor mat or rug in the bathroom, but never anything around the toilet. We don't do toilet ring rugs or toilet seat covers anymore, they're dated and hide a lot of germs, which makes people uncomfortable.

The other option for a guest bathroom can be something small like the guest bathroom for kids that are coming in and out. So it might be a half bath that's off the basement or the kitchen. In that instance, you don't need to do anything major. I would have two hand towels, some liquid soap, possibly something on the floor and then maybe just some simple art on the walls.

All bathrooms need to have Kleenex and toilet paper. Clients will use the bathroom so you may as well make it comfortable for them because if they like the house well enough to use the bathroom, it tells you that they're comfortable in the home, which is really very, very important.

Pull the first tissue slightly out of the box and always create a triangle with the edge of the toilet paper. The details will help to sell your home.

So, again, follow the same steps. Who's this bathroom for? What are my anchor and foundation? How can I create a full and complete scene and a little added pocket of emotion? Imagine pulling back the shower curtain and seeing 25 rubber ducks; it would absolutely tickle your funny bone. Follow the six steps. How do you know they're working? Number one, people will use the bathroom, which is fine, just make sure you freshen it up every once in a while. Kids will walk out holding a rubber duck. That way you know it's worked because they've interacted with the scene. Once again, you have a variety of ways to stage with love no matter what type of home it is, no matter who the bathroom is for.

Components for a great family bath scene:

- 1 set of towels
- Shower Curtain, Rod, rings and liner
- 25 rubber ducks
- Floor mat
- Tissues, toilet paper
- Toothpaste, toothbrush, toothbrush holder

Hot Tips on getting every home buyer to fall in love with your house

1) **POE's in a kids bath** can be as simple as a rubber duck or Barbie toothbrush
2) Use local décor in a guest bath to make your **guest feel welcome** and at home

You know its working when **people use the bathroom**

Chapter Eleven
Leaving with Love

Leaving with Love for the new home buyer

If you've done your job and started by defining your customer, making certain that your marketing spoke to your specific customer, you connected the dots between your customer, the marketing, the staging and the home and you have staged with true love in every room of the house, your home will sell very, very quickly and very effectively. Now your job is to leave the home with love. So, first and foremost, figure out what else you need to do to this home.

Ask yourself, "What can I do with this home without spending a dime? Many times it means that you've been able to clean up, clean out, rearrange and give the home a new fresh feel without ever spending any money. You might not have realized how to put a full scene together or how to add a Pockets of Emotion® or how to clean something up so that it looked fresh and new and it didn't cost you anything, except for just a little bit of your time and a little bit of elbow grease.

When you do stage with love with full scenes and Pockets of Emotion® that speak directly to your customer, you will achieve the global results that we achieve each and every day at Simple Appeal®, Inc. and APSD®.

Now, here's the best part. These scenes can go with you or you can leave something extra special for the new buyer. What I normally do is to leave the home with 'unadvertised' love, so I'll usually leave one staged room which, generally speaking, is a bathroom so that when they move in they already have a complete bathroom with a shower curtain, a nice set of towels, some tissue, toilet paper, hand soap and one special local memento.

It may be that it's the kids' bathroom and so they have a tub full of rubber ducks, little rubber duck hand towels and two yellow toothbrushes and that's okay too. Normally, I will leave love with that room because it gets them started right away. Moving can be very stressful, so whenever you do that they immediately feel loved and know that they made the right choice.

The other thing you should do is leave them what I refer to as a 'love note.' That means that you should write them a letter and say thank you so much for moving into what's now their home. You might mention how many years you lived there, that you loved the house and loved the neighbors. List some of the special things, whether it is a bike trail, schools, churches, specific things about your property, your swimming pool and tell them what those things meant to you. Then simply say you hope they mean the same for them. Tell them to enjoy their new home and then sign it with Great Love, the Smith Family.

There you go. That's leaving a home with love, leaving them one room that they can enjoy, move into right away and use and a love letter.

By putting some research, focus and love into prepping your home for sale, you will find that you are able to sell in half the time at full market value. At Simple Appeal®, along with our global team of APSD® home staging professionals are currently able to get homes under contract in as little as one day with our current average being 21 Days on market.

If you are ready to sell quickly and need help, give our office a call for a home stager referral in your area or an online service. 1-877-900-STAGE.

In the meantime, get out there a sell your home with a little love!

*** In order to get access to our free Online Staging Photo Portfolio, simply go to: **www.SimpleAppeal.com/PhotoPortfolio**

Chapter Twelve
Resources & Checklists

Photo Examples: **www.SimpleAppeal.com/PhotoPortfolio**

Home Staging Training and Certification- **www.APSDmembers.com** / 1-877-900-STAGE

Home Staging and Consultation- **www.SimpleAppeal.com** or 1-888-900-2872

Open House Events- **www.SimpleAppeal.com** / **Info@SimpleAppeal.com**

To book Karen as a Speaker- **www.SimpleAppeal.com** and click on the 'Book Karen as a Speaker menu button' or call 1-888-900-2872

Home Staging Training Events- **www.APSDmembers.com/STAGE**
Join Karen Schaefer and her Home Staging Dream Team for this LIVE 3 day home staging, business and marketing training event. It is the only one like it in the world!

Checklist* #1 – *Working with Real Estate Agents*

How to best work with your real estate agent to create a win-win relationship

1) **Make sure you have found the right agent for you**
    - How many houses have they listed and sold in the past 90 days?
    - How many were like yours and in your price range?
    - How many were in your area?
    - What will he or she do to specifically focus directly on the sale of your home?

2) **Be clear about your goals, pricing and timeline and come to a mutual agreement on these points with your agent.**
    - What are your specific goals with the transaction of your home?
    - What is the timeframe in which you need this house sold?
    - How much do you want to sell it for? Is that realistic?
    - What is your bottom line? Can she make that happen?
    - What needs to be done, point by point, in your home in order to get it sold in the shortest amount of time for the most amount of money?

3) **Create your marketing plan**
    - What is the marketing plan the agent will offer you?
    - What is the timeline for the plan?
    - How will you be able to see the marketing?

- How will it be tracked?
- How will adjustments be made if needed?
- Are there any extraordinary marketing efforts the agent is willing to offer?
- What are the advertising options?
- How will you be promoted on Social Media?
- What offline and online marketing will your agent give you? When? How often?
- Is there an Open House and if so when? How will it be different than other open houses so you can attract the most amount of potential buyers?
- What can you do to help the agent sell your home in terms of home preparation, marketing and support?

4) **Develop a Cycle of Communication and Action**
   - How often will you hear from your agent? (At least every 2 weeks regardless of showings is reasonable)
   - When will they contact you with feedback from each showing and how? (You want the feedback from every single showing so you know what needs to be improved)
   - How will they let you know what needs to be updated, changed or cleaned according to the feedback?
   - What are you willing to do in order to follow the advice of your agent and get your home sold in the shortest amount of time for the most amount of money?

Checklist* #2 – Working with Real Estate Investors

How to best work with your real estate investor to sell your home quickly

1) Make sure you have found the right real estate investor with your best interest in mind
   - Why do you want to work with this investor?
   - Why is this the right investor for you?
   - Have you checked their referrals?
   - Are they willing to close with an attorney?
   - Will they put everything in writing and have it notarized?

2) Be clear about your goals, pricing and timeline and come to a mutual agreement on these points with the real estate investor
   - What exit strategy will the investor employ?
   - In what timeframe?
   - For what amount of money?
   - When will you get your money?
   - Is it guaranteed? How?
   - Will you still be on the loan, if so, for how long?
   - What happens if they can't execute the transaction?
   - What will you need to do to the home to help speed up the successful sale?

3) **Create your marketing plan**
    - What is the marketing plan the investor will implement?
    - What is the timeline for the plan?
    - Do they have a list of potential buyers?
    - Will you have to move out in order for them to transact the property?
    - What can you do to help?

4) **Develop a Cycle of Communication and Action**
    - How often will you hear from the investor?
    - When will they contact you with feedback and timelines?
    - How can you reach them?
    - What actions are you willing to take in order to successfully transact your home?
    - What actions are they willing to take in order to successfully transact your home?

Checklist* #3 – How to Best Sell your Home as a FSBO

How to best sell your home as a FSBO

1) **Why are you selling on your own?**
    - ➢ Upside down on your mortgage?
    - ➢ Don't trust agents or investors?
    - ➢ You already have the experience to do so?
    - ➢ Not enough equity to use someone else?

2) **Have a clear vision on your goals, pricing and timeline.**
    - ➢ Are you willing to offer multiple exit strategies?
    - ➢ Can you carry the financing?
    - ➢ How did you come up with your price? Have you researched other similar homes and their 'sold' prices within the past 90 days?
    - ➢ How fast would you like to sell?
    - ➢ Are you willing to use a closing attorney and title company? (depending upon the legal structure in your county and state)
    - ➢ What are you willing to do in order to get your home sold within the guidelines of your goals?

3) **Create your marketing plan**
    - ➢ What is the marketing plan you will implement?
    - ➢ What is the timeline for the plan?
    - ➢ How many signs, flyers, postcards and ads will you place, where and when?

- Will you host an Open House? If so, when and what will you do in order to make it a success?
- Who can help you implement your marketing plan for a successful sale?

4) **Develop a Cycle of Communication and Action with your prospects**
   - How often will you follow up with a caller or viewer?
   - How will you collect and maintain the prospects contact information? (Follow the checklist* provided)
   - What questions will you ask with the follow up? (you need to get their honest feedback, so the best thing to ask is just that; "If you were going to put an offer in on this home today, what would you tell me you love about it and what would you like to change? How much would you offer me?)
   - What actions or terms are you willing to take in order to successfully transact your home?

> ## Checklist* #4 – Contact Questionnaire

Contact Questionnaire

1) What can I answer for you? (Always ask them first vs. jumping right into the benefits. This way you can speak directly to their wants and desires instead of guessing what may appeal to them.)

2) Just in case we get cut off, can I get your name and phone number?

3) Would you like me to mail or email you further information? Great, what is your email/mail address?

4) What is important to you about this home?

5) If you knew your price range, what would it be?

6) When is the best time for you and your family to see the home, Morning or evening? Friday or Saturday?

Checklist* #5 – Overall Property Condition

Check List

First Impression of Exterior/Curb Appeal: _____
_____
_____
_____

Condition of:

House Paint
    Front _____
    Back _____
    Sides _____
    Deck _____
    Railing _____
    Garage Door _____
    Front Door/Rear Door _____
    Trim _____
    Lighting _____

Yard
    Clean _____
    Grass-even _____
    Grading _____
    Shrubs _____
    Flowers/Beds _____
    Garden _____
    Drainage _____
    Window Wells _____
    Mailbox _____

Checklist* #5 – Overall Property Condition

Decks/Patios
    Boards _____
    Railing _____
    Stain _____
    Nails _____
    Steps _____
    Landings _____
    Supports _____

Structure
    Foundation _____
    Siding _____
    Bricks _____
    Wood _____
    Trim _____
    Gutters/Down Spouts _____
    Windows _____
    Roof _____

Storage Units
    Roof _____
    Structure _____
    Electric _____
    Heat _____
    Windows _____
    Siding _____
    Paint _____
    Clean _____
    Transportable _____

Checklist* #5 – Overall Property Condition

Fencing
    Wood _____

    Wire _____

    Gates _____

    Closures _____

    Stain _____

    Supports _____

Notes:
_____
_____
_____
_____
_____
_____
_____
_____
_____
_____

First Impression of Interior of Property: _____
_____
_____
_____

Condition of:

Kitchen
    Layout _____

    Walls _____

    Ceiling _____

Checklist* #5 – Overall Property Condition

Kitchen (cont.)
Floors _____

Outlets _____

Windows _____

    Panes _____

    Coverings _____

    Ledges _____

    Wells _____

Vents _____

Doors _____

Knobs _____

Paint _____

Lighting _____

Heat _____

Cabinets _____

Refrigerator _____

Stove/Oven _____

Microwave _____

Range Hood _____

Dishwasher _____

Garbage Disposal _____

Sinks _____

Counter Tops _____

Fixtures _____

Ceiling Fan _____

Ventilation _____

Cabinet knobs _____

Drawer Pulls _____

Checklist* #5 – Overall Property Condition

Family Room
Layout _____
Walls _____
Ceiling _____
Floors _____
Outlets _____
Windows _____
    Panes _____
    Coverings _____
    Ledges _____
    Wells _____
Vents _____
Doors _____
Knobs _____
Paint _____
Lighting _____
Heat _____
Ceiling Fans _____
Fireplace/Wood Stove _____

Dining Room
Layout _____
Walls _____
Ceiling _____
Floors _____
Outlets _____
Windows _____
    Panes _____
    Coverings _____
    Ledges _____

Checklist* #5 – Overall Property Condition

Dining Room (cont.)

Vents _____
Doors _____
Knobs _____
Paint _____
Lighting _____
Heat _____
Ceiling Fans _____

Living Room

Layout _____
Walls _____
Ceiling _____
Floors _____
Outlets _____
Windows _____
    Panes _____
    Coverings _____
    Ledges _____
Vents _____
Doors (Coat Closet) _____
Knobs _____
Paint _____
Lighting _____
Heat _____
Ceiling Fans _____
Fireplace/Wood Stove _____

LoveSellsBook.com
by Karen Schaefer

Checklist* #5 – Overall Property Condition

Bedroom #_____

Layout _____
Walls _____
Ceiling _____
Floors _____
Outlets _____
Windows _____
    Panes _____
    Coverings _____
    Ledges _____
    Wells _____
Vents _____
Doors _____
Knobs _____
Paint _____
Lighting _____
Heat _____
Door _____
Knob _____
Closet Doors _____
Knobs _____

Bedroom #_____

Layout _____
Walls _____
Ceiling _____
Floors _____
Outlets _____

Checklist* #5 – Overall Property Condition

Bedroom #_____ (cont.)
Windows
    Panes
    Coverings
    Ledges
    Wells
Vents
Doors
Knobs
Paint
Lighting
Heat
Door
Knob
Closet Doors
Knobs

Bedroom #_____
Layout
Walls
Ceiling
Floors
Outlets
Windows
    Panes
    Coverings
    Ledges
    Wells
Vents

Checklist* #5 – Overall Property Condition

Bedroom # _____ (cont.)
Doors _____
Knobs _____
Paint _____
Lighting _____
Heat _____
Door _____
Knob _____
Closet Doors _____
Knobs _____

Bath # _____
Layout _____
Walls _____
Ceiling _____
Floors _____
Outlets _____
Windows _____
    Panes _____
    Coverings _____
    Ledges _____
    Wells _____
Vents _____
Doors _____
Knobs _____
Paint _____
Lighting _____
Heat _____
Tubs _____
Toilets _____

Checklist* #5 — Overall Property Condition

Bath # _____ (cont.)

Shower Curtain _____
Sink _____
Vanity _____
Mirror _____
Fixtures
    Sink _____
    Tub/Shower _____
Door _____
Knob _____
Drawer Pulls _____
Linen Closet _____
Grout _____
Caulking _____
Toilet Seat _____

Bath # _____

Layout _____
Walls _____
Ceiling _____
Floors _____
Outlets _____
Windows _____
    Panes _____
    Coverings _____
    Ledges _____
    Wells _____
Vents _____
Doors _____

Checklist* #5 – Overall Property Condition

Bath # _____ (cont.)

Knobs
Paint
Lighting
Heat
Tubs
Toilets
Shower Curtain
Sink
Vanity
Mirror
Fixtures
   Sink
   Tub/Shower
Door
Knob
Drawer Pulls
Linen Closet
Grout
Caulking
Toilet Seat

Office

Layout
Walls
Ceiling
Floors
Outlets

Checklist* #5 – Overall Property Condition

Office (cont.)

Windows
    Panes
    Coverings
    Ledges
    Wells
Vents
Doors
Knobs
Paint
Lighting
Heat

Basement

Layout
Walls
Ceiling
Floors
Outlets
Windows
    Panes
    Coverings
    Ledges
    Wells
Vents
Doors
Knobs
Paint
Lighting

Checklist* #5 – Overall Property Condition

Basement (cont.)
Heat _____
Stairs _____
Fireplace/Wood Stove _____
Finished _____
Rough-In _____

Garage
Layout _____
Walls _____
Ceiling _____
Floors _____
Outlets _____
Windows _____
    Panes _____
    Coverings _____
    Ledges _____
    Wells _____
Vents _____
Doors _____
Knobs _____
Paint _____
Lighting _____
Heat _____
Door to/from House _____
Drainage _____
Heat _____

Checklist* #5 – Overall Property Condition

Utilities

Hot Water Heater _____

Base board heating
units in each room _____

Temperature Controls _____

Thermostat _____

Heater (and filters) _____

Air Conditioner _____

Water Softener
(and filters) _____

Washer/Dryer _____

Radon Filters _____

Speakers _____

Security System _____

Notes: _____

_____

_____

_____

_____

_____

_____

_____

_____

_____

_____

_____

_____

_____

_____

_____

Checklist* #6 – Cleaning your Home for Sale

Utilities:

Some utilities will require cleaning and servicing. It is best to do this prior to putting your home on the market as you will offset any potential problems that may come up during inspection. It also gives the appearance of a clean and well maintained home.

Hot Water Heater, cleaned and serviced
Air Conditioner, cleaned and serviced
Furnace, cleaned and serviced
Ducts, cleaned
Vents, cleaned

Home Features and Structures:

Fireplaces
Inside
Outside
Above, Below
Hearth, Mantle
Chute
Wood Holder
Utensils

Jacuzzi's/Steam Room
Date of Service
Fresh water and treatments
Cleaned walls, ceiling and floor
Fresh smell
Dry walking area

Windows:
Glass inside and out
Window Frames
Window locks
Tracks

Remove screens, clean and place in garage
Touch up paint if necessary
Clean sills
Clean, Steam or wash window treatments

Walls, Ceilings, Trim:
Wash all walls, paint where necessary
Scrub all ceilings where needed, especially above a fireplace
Touch up ceiling paint where needed
Wash all door, ceiling, window and floor trim
Touch up paint where necessary
Remove all cobwebs and dust bunnies

Doors:
Wash all doors
Touch up paint where necessary
Patch any holes or replace door if needed
Wash around all door handles along with the handles
Replace any door handles that do not match the other metals within a line of sight
All handles should match all hinges
Replace painted hinges unless home is being sold wholesale
Make sure doors open and close easily and effortlessly

Light Fixtures:
Make sure all metals are appropriate for room and color of other metals within the room
Replace all bulbs
Clean light fixture globe
Clean ceiling fan blades

Light Switches and Switch Plates:
Plates and Plugs need to match
Wipe down all plates and switches

LoveSellsBook.com
by Karen Schaefer

Floors:
Wash all hard surfaces and if appropriate treat them with murphy's oil, bona, or wax
Vacuum daily
Have rugs professionally cleaned along with any area rugs
Clean corners with an attachment to avoid dust build up

Appliances:
Clean inside and out of all appliances:
Toaster Oven
Microwave
Oven
Stove
Refrigerator and top of refrigerator
Coffee Maker
Tea Pot
Juicer
Garbage Disposal
Warmer/Steamer
Turn on self cleaning oven, wipe out when cool
Clean oven hood outside and underneath
Remove all fingerprints, daily
Scrub inside of refrigerator, and remove any strong odors
Add Baking soda box to fridge and freezer

Kitchens:
Clean sinks, plugs and drains
Run garbage disposal and trash compactor daily
Remove trash daily and wash out trash can to remove smell
Clean out under sink and organize
Empty dishwasher daily
Remove all non-daily appliances from countertop
Leave only 1-2 tea towels out at any given time and only if they are clean
Put away all food except fresh herbs or fresh fruit that is displayed in a bowl

Bathrooms:
Scrub Bathtub with appropriate cleaner so there is no soap ring or mildew
Recaulk tub, sink and toilet
Windex all mirrors and fixtures
Clean Sink and vanity top
Clean entire toilet, inside and out
Replace shower curtain liner with a clear frosted liner
Clean shower doors, handles and tracks
Organize beneath sink or cabinets

Checklist* #7 – Daily Staging for Occupied Homes

Give each person in your family a checklist* and assign them to the room, scene or clean up task on a daily or weekly basis until the home is sold. Follow this list on a daily basis since you never know when you will have a buyer.

Kitchen
Remove all 'extra appliances' and place them under the sink, in a cabinet if there is room or in a large Rubbermaid bin and set it neatly in the garage.
Pull out your appropriate 'scene' and set it up.
Wipe down all counter tops
Wash and put away dishes
Empty Trash cans
Clean off kitchen table and add simple centerpiece (flowers, bowl of candy, etc.)
Sweep floor

Bathrooms
Remove all towels, floor mats, messy soaps, shampoos, and toiletries and place them under the sink or in a Rubbermaid bin neatly in the garage.
Pull out the appropriate staging 'scene' for each bathroom and display in each bathroom.
Wipe out tub, sink and vanity top.
Windex mirror and faucet.
Make sure toilet is clean and usable
Fold toilet paper in triangle
Add a box of tissues to the bathroom
Empty trash can a put in a new liner

Bedrooms
Make beds, fluff pillows
Put away extra toys, homework and knickknacks
If appropriate place 'scene in room'
Pick up dirty clothes and place in laundry room hamper
Vacuum
Empty Trash

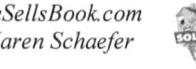

Pets

Place pet, food, toys and bed in a secure area in case of showings
Wipe pet down with pet wipes to ensure a neutral scent
Give pet a good run or walk for the day as a tired and happy pet leads to a better showing

Clean Up

Dishes should be cleaned and put away. Empty dishwasher if possible.
Wipe down common door handle areas such as the bathroom, front and back doors
Remove smudges and fingerprints from appliances and glass doors
Empty all trash
Sweep all floors
Run Vacuum
All dirty clothes should be out of sight
Open curtains and blinds equal distance so they look good from the inside and out
Set out all scene's and POE's.

Checklist* #8 – 6 Steps to Staging

1) **Define your Buyer-** Before you prep you home for sale, look around see who else is buying homes in your neighborhood, do your research and prep the home for the right buyer.

2) **CCTF-** Color, Continuity, Theme and Flow. These should work together within each room and then throughout the house to give the home the right 'feel'

3) **Foundation-** all pieces of a scene must come together on a common foundation in order to get a sense of a full and complete scene. This might be on a table, a rug or any surface that pulls the scene together

4) **Anchor-** One fixed or added piece within a room that pulls focus from the rest of the room to this particular area or piece. This helps in being able to focus your staging efforts primarily on the anchor

5) **Scenes-** This is something you want to create in most rooms of the house in order to attract your buyer and give them the sense that this home is specifically for them.

6) **POE-** Pockets of Emotion® are the single best selling secret you have when it comes to selling your home quickly. These are the moments in the house that let someone get emotional, build a connection, tickles their funny bone and reminisce about great memories

Checklist* #9 – Marketing

Signs
Theme the signs if possible (depends upon when you sell but you might theme them with footballs for super bowl season, flowers for spring, wreaths for Christmas and so on.)
Sign in Front Yard
Sign at entrance to Street (Both sides if possible)
Sign at entrance to Subdivision (Both sides if possible)
Directional signs at nearest intersection/cross street

Flyers
Flyers at the bottom of signs
Flyers posted in all community areas such as schools, churches, grocery stores, Laundromats, etc.
Flyers distributed to all local small businesses
Flyers distributed to all networking outlets (Friends, teachers, postman, pastor, etc.)

Post cards
Used to invite the neighborhood to a private showing (because they will tell their friends and family)
Send to 'Farm' area (discus a farm area with your agent) every 30 days
Use in any bag give-aways at local grocery stores, schools, church events, farmers markets, etc.
Use as a 'business card' when you want to tell people about it

Offline and Online Ads
Craigs List Posting
Local Community Paper
Posting on your agents site
FSBO posting sites
Local publications, newsletters and bulletins

> Checklist* #10 – Curb Appeal

APSD® Curb Appeal Consultation Checklist

Metals Match
- ☐ Lights
- ☐ Door handles
- ☐ Door bell or Knocker

Exterior Paint Color and Condition
- ☐ Current Color Trend
- ☐ Good Condition on House Color
- ☐ Good Condition on Front Door Color
- ☐ Good Condition on Garage Door
- ☐ Good Condition on Trim

Inside from the Outside
- ☐ Blinds all at equal level on inside
- ☐ Cutain's pulled equal distance on inside
- ☐ Window Sills are uncluttered
- ☐ Window Screens are removed
- ☐ Windows are clean
- ☐ Interior looks good from Exterior

Front Door
- ☐ Condition
- ☐ Color
- ☐ Appropriate for Home/Neighborhood

Yard/Garden
- ☐ Mowed and Trimmed
- ☐ Edged
- ☐ Trees/Hedges/Bushes Trimmed
- ☐ Trash Removed/Out of Sight
- ☐ Mailbox Condition
- ☐ Flower Garden
- ☐ Plant at Front Door
- ☐ Neighbor's Yard OK
- ☐ Pocket of Emotion™

Feature Area
- ☐ View
- ☐ Sitting Area
- ☐ Play Area
- ☐ Pool/Hot Tub
- ☐ Flowers
- ☐ Pocket of Emotion™

Marketing
- ☐ Signs
- ☐ Themed Decor
- ☐ DIrectional Signs Sponsors
- ☐ Atractors/Workers
- ☐ Flowers
- ☐ Pocket of Emotion™

Additional Comments and Suggestions:
_____
_____
_____
_____
_____
_____
_____

Dear Reader,

Thank you for investing in **'Love Sells; How to get every home buyer to fall in love with your house.'**

If I can help you sell your home, listing or investment property faster, or consult with you on how to turn your existing property into a cash-producing investment, please feel free to contact me at the information provided below.

We will also be happy to discuss our globally recognized APSD Home Staging Training and Certification programs.

Thank you!

Karen

Karen Schaefer

If you are interested in home staging, home design or consultation services you can contact **Support@SimpleAppeal.com.**

For information on becoming an APSD® Certified Home Stager or Home Staging Trainer, email **Membership@APSDmembers.com** or call 1-877-900-STAGE

To inquire into Consultation, Coaching or Booking Karen as a Speaker, call: 1-888-900-2872 or email **Karen@SimpleAppeal.com**

The End
(That's for you Dad!)

www.LoveSellsBook.com

P.O.Box 271 | Manitou Springs, CO 80829 | 1-877-900-STAGE

LoveSellsBook.com
by Karen Schaefer

Coming Soon!

Whether you decide to sell your home or keep it, there is always a way to make money on your real estate investments. Karen's next book will show you how to turn your exiting home, a new investment or current rental into a real estate cash flow machine!

**'Vacation Rentals;
How to pay your entire year's mortgage in just 4 weeks'!**

To find out more details go to: www.LoveSellsBook.com

www.ingramcontent.com/pod-product-compliance
Lightning Source LLC
Chambersburg PA
CBHW071012200526
45171CB00007B/67